GIVING

nlocking
the heart
of good
tewardship

GIVING

locking
the heart
of good
ewardship

JOHN ORTBERG,
LAURIE PEDERSON,
JUDSON POLING

PURSUING SPIRITUAL TRANSFORMATION

WILLOW
Willow Creek Resources

ZONDERVAN™

GRAND RAPIDS, MICHIGAN 49530 USA

We want to hear from you. Please send your comments about this book to us in care of zreview@zondervan.com. Thank you.

ZONDERVAN™

Giving: Unlocking the Heart of Good Stewardship
Copyright © 2000 by the Willow Creek Association

Requests for information should be addressed to:

Zondervan, *Grand Rapids, Michigan 49530*

ISBN 0-310-22078-5

We are grateful for permission given by a number of gifted teachers to use excerpts from their books and messages for the opening readings in the sessions. These authors and speakers are acknowledged throughout this guide.

Interior design by Laura Klynstra Blost

Printed in the United States of America

07 08 09 /❖ EP/ 18 17 16 15 14

CONTENTS

118223

Pursuing Spiritual Transformation

The Pursuing Spiritual Transformation series is all about being spiritual. But that may not mean what you think!

Do you consider yourself a spiritual person? What does that mean? Does spiritual growth seem like an impossible amount of work? Do you have a clear picture of the kind of life you'd live if you were to be more spiritual?

Each guide in the Pursuing Spiritual Transformation series is dedicated to one thing—helping you pursue authentic spiritual transformation. In this guide the focus is growing through the biblical stewardship of your money and possessions. (Certainly, good stewardship also extends to our time, talents, and spiritual gifts. Those aspects are explored in another book of this series, *Gifts: The Joy of Serving God*.)

You may find this study different from others you have done in the past. Each week in preparation for your group meeting, you will be completing a Bible study and experimenting with a variety of spiritual exercises. These elements are designed to enhance your private times with God and, in turn, to help you invite him into all aspects of your life, even the everyday routines. After all, spiritual life is just *life*—the one you live moment by moment.

It is very important that you complete this work before going to each meeting because the discussion is based on what you've learned from the study and what you've observed as a result of the spiritual exercise. The Bible study and exercise are not meant to be done an hour before the meeting, quickly filling in the blanks. Instead, we suggest you thoughtfully and prayerfully complete them over the course of several days as part of your regular devotional time with God.

A good modern Bible translation, such as the New International Version, the New American Standard Bible, or the New Revised

Standard Version, will give you the most help in your study. You might also consider keeping a Bible dictionary handy to look up unfamiliar words, names, or places. Write your responses in the spaces provided in the study guide or use your personal journal if you need more space. This will help you participate more fully in the discussion, and will also help you personalize what you are learning.

When your group meets, be willing to join in the discussion. The leader of the group will not be lecturing but will encourage people to discuss what they have learned from the study and exercise. Plan to share what God has taught you. Try to be sensitive to the other members of the group. Listen attentively when they speak, and be affirming whenever you can. This will encourage more hesitant members of the group to participate. Be careful not to dominate the discussion. By all means participate, but allow others to have equal time. If you are a group leader or a participant who wants further insights, you will find additional commments in the Leader's Guide at the back of the study.

We believe that your ongoing journey through this material will place you on an exciting path of spiritual adventure. Through your individual study time and group discussions, we trust you will enter into a fresh concept of spiritual life that will delight the heart of God . . . and your heart too!

Ten Core Values
for Spiritual Formation

Spiritual transformation . . .

    . . . is essential, not optional, for Christ-followers.

    . . . is a process, not an event.

    . . . is God's work, but requires my participation.

    . . . involves those practices, experiences, and relationships that help me live intimately with Christ and walk as if he were in my place.

    . . . is not a compartmentalized pursuit. God is not interested in my spiritual life; he's interested in my *life*—all of it.

    . . . can happen in every moment. It is not restricted to certain times or practices.

    . . . is not individualistic, but takes place in community and finds expression in serving others.

    . . . is not impeded by a person's background, temperament, life situation, or season of life. It is available right now to all who desire it.

    . . . and the means of pursuing it will vary from one individual to another. Fully devoted followers are handcrafted, not mass-produced.

    . . . is ultimately gauged by an increased capacity to love God and people. Superficial or external checklists cannot measure it.

Giving: Unlocking the Heart of Good Stewardship

While he was in Bethany, reclining at the table in the home of a man known as Simon the Leper, a woman came with an alabaster jar of very expensive perfume, made of pure nard. She broke the jar and poured the perfume on his head.

Some of those present were saying indignantly to one another, "Why this waste of perfume? It could have been sold for more than a year's wages and the money given to the poor." And they rebuked her harshly.

"Leave her alone," said Jesus. "Why are you bothering her? She has done a beautiful thing to me. The poor you will always have with you, and you can help them any time you want. But you will not always have me. She did what she could. She poured perfume on my body beforehand to prepare for my burial. I tell you the truth, wherever the gospel is preached throughout the world, what she has done will also be told, in memory of her."

—Mark 14:3–9

Of all the acts of servanthood he witnessed, one touched Jesus' heart so deeply that he memorialized it forever. One would expect the spotlight of his attention to fall on some grand sacrifice, something of "high impact." But what left Christ's heart pierced was a woman named Mary and her alabaster jar.

An alabaster jar. We all have one. They come in different shapes and sizes, and sealed within is all that we prize—our treasured earthly possessions. Occasionally we break the seal, remove the lid and share—as we know we ought. But we do so carefully, reservedly, with control, anxious all the while to put the lid back on. So much of life is spent preserving and conserving what we hold in our alabaster jar.

Mary's servanthood brings each of us to a fork in the road. The question of good stewardship—What will you do with your alabaster jar?—is one that every person must decide.

Ultimately, good stewardship is not a matter of wise money management or even responsible giving. It is a matter of extravagant love. Have you taken in the love of Christ extravagantly poured out for you? Has it left your heart so filled with gratitude that you can't help but lavishly pour it out in return? Is his love transforming your prayers from "Give me, Lord" to "Use me, Lord—all that I am and all that I hold dear"?

In the words of author Ken Gire, "The Savior had come to earth to break an alabaster jar for humanity. And Mary had come that night to break one for him.

"It was a jar he never regretted breaking. Nor did she."

Nor will you.

SESSION
ONE

MONEY: WHY IS IT SO
IMPORTANT TO GOD?

Money: Why Is It So Important to God?

Reading adapted from *Money, Possessions and Eternity*, by Randy Alcorn

Were I the Bible's editor, I would cut out much of what it says about money and possessions. Anyone can see it devotes a disproportionate amount of space to a subject of secondary importance. When it comes to money and possessions, the Bible is sometimes redundant, often extreme, and occasionally shocking.

And, after all, we come to the Bible for comfort—not for a lecture on finances. If we want to know about money, we can go to *Fortune, Forbes*, or the *Wall Street Journal*. Scripture should concern itself with the spiritual and heavenly. Money is physical and earthly. The Bible is religious; money is secular. Let God talk about love and grace and brotherhood, thank you. Let the rest of us talk about money and possessions.

For serious Christians some hard questions are in order here. How *could* the Bible's Author and Editor justify devoting twice as many verses to money than to faith and prayer combined? And how could Jesus say more about money than both heaven and hell? Didn't he know what was really important?

The sheer enormity of Scripture's teaching on this subject screams for our attention. And the haunting and immensely important question is, *why?* Why did the Savior of the world say more about how we are to view and handle

Why did the Savior of the world say more about how we are to view and handle money and possessions than about any other single thing?

money and possessions than about any other single thing? Why?

Money and Conversion

The enigma deepens when we look at how closely Jesus linked money to salvation itself. When Zacchaeus said he would give half his money to the poor and pay back four times over those he had cheated, Jesus did not merely say, "Good idea." He said, "Today salvation has come to this house" (Luke 19:9). This is amazing. Jesus judged the reality of this man's salvation based on his willingness, no, his cheerful *eagerness* to part with his money for the glory of God and the good of others.

Zacchaeus is not an isolated case. When his audience asked John the Baptist what they should do to bear the fruit of repentance, first he told them to share their clothes and food with the poor. Then he told the tax collectors not to collect and pocket extra money. And finally he told the soldiers not to extort money and to be content with their wages (Luke 3:7–14). In all three cases, the conclusive proof of a spiritual change was an altered perspective on the handling of money and possessions.

In Mark 12 we meet a poor widow. She put in the temple offering box two tiny copper coins, worth a fraction of a penny. This was the only money she had. Jesus called his disciples together to teach them a lesson from the woman. Did he question the wisdom of her actions? Did he say she should have been more sensible? No, he gave her an unqualified commendation for her choice: "I tell you the truth, this poor widow has put more into the treasury than all the others. They all gave out of their wealth; but she, out of her poverty, put in everything—all she had to live on" (vv. 43–44). Jesus enshrined her example in the Word of God that all believers in the future might emulate her faith, commitment, and sacrificial generosity.

To liquidate and disperse cheerfully the assets one had spent a lifetime accumulating was no more natural then than now. And that is the whole point. Conversion and

The conclusive proof of a spiritual change was an altered perspective on the handling of money and possessions.

the filling of the Holy Spirit were supernatural experiences that produced supernatural responses. While there was still the private ownership of property, the joyful giving and sharing of this property became the new "norm" of supernatural living.

If a first-century Christian were to visit us today and gauge *our* spiritual condition by our attitudes and actions regarding money and possessions, what conclusions would he come to?

The Story Money Tells

Money is a litmus test of our true character. It is an index of our spiritual life. Our stewardship of money tells a deep and consequential story. It forms our biography. In a sense, how we relate to money and possessions is the story of our lives.

Money is a litmus test of our true character.

If this is true of all men in all ages, does it not have special application to us who live in a time and place of unparalleled affluence? Take a man or woman who works from age twenty-five to sixty-five and makes $15,000 a year. In his lifetime this person of modest income by our standards will handle well over half a million dollars. He will manage a fortune. And if Scripture is true, and men must give an account of their lives to God (Rom. 14:12), then one day this man must answer these questions: Where did it all go? What did I spend it on? What has been accomplished for eternity through my use of all this wealth?

In the account of the poor widow, Mark wrote, "Jesus sat down opposite the place where the offerings were put and watched the crowd putting their money into the temple treasury" (Mark 12:41).

Notice we are not told, "Jesus happened to see . . . ." No, it seems he deliberately *watched* to observe what people were giving.

Jesus was interested enough in who was giving what to make an immediate object lesson to the disciples about the true nature of trusting God as demonstrated in sacrificial financial giving.

If we stop to think about it, this passage makes all of us who suppose that what we do with our money is our business and only our business feel terribly uncomfortable. On the contrary, it is painfully apparent that it is *God's* business—that God makes it his business. He does not apologize for watching with intense interest what we do with the money he has entrusted to us. If we use our imaginations, we might even peer into the invisible realm to see him gathering some of his subjects together this very moment. Perhaps you can hear him using *your* handling of finances as an object lesson. The question is, what kind of lesson?

Getting Close to Home

Sometimes more is to be learned from the passages of Scripture we avoid or skim over than those we underline or post on our refrigerator. The Bible contains an arsenal of such verses on the subject of money and possessions, and they just keep firing away at us.

The more we allow ourselves to grapple with these unsettling passages, the more we are pierced. Our only options, it seems, are to let Christ wound us until he accomplishes what he wishes, *or* to avoid his words and his gaze and his presence altogether by staying away from his Word. The latter option is easier in the short run. But no true disciple can really be content with it.

By now some readers are long gone and others who remain are uncomfortable. I must admit that I share your discomfort. You may even be thinking, "I'd rather not deal with these issues. I'm content doing what I'm doing." But are you *really* content? Are any of us who know Christ, who have his Spirit within, really content when we haven't fully considered his words? When we haven't completely opened ourselves to what he has for us? Comfortable, perhaps. Complacent, certainly. But not content.

I, for one, hate to live with that nagging feeling deep inside that when Jesus called people to follow him he had more in mind than I'm experiencing. I don't want to miss

I, for one, hate to live with that nagging feeling deep inside that when Jesus called people to follow him he had more in mind than I'm experiencing.

out on what he has for me. If he has really touched your life, I don't think you do either.

For all these sobering implications, I must quickly add that for me the process of discovering God's will about money and possessions, rather than being burdensome, has been tremendously liberating. My own growth and enlightenment in financial stewardship has closely paralleled my overall spiritual growth. In fact, it has *propelled* it. I have learned more about faith, trust, grace, commitment, and God's provision in this arena than in any other.

I have also learned why Paul said, "God loves a cheerful giver," and I have found that a cheerful giver loves God, and loves him more deeply each time he gives. To me, one of the few experiences comparable to the joy of leading someone to Christ is the joy of making wise and generous choices with my money. Both are supreme acts of worship. Both are what we were made for.

I write not as a critic or crusader but as an excited learner. I feel like a child who has found a wonderful trail hidden in the woods—a trail that countless others have blazed but one which seems to the child to be as new and fresh as if it had never before existed. The exhilaration of this adventure is impossible to describe. It can only be experienced.

A cheerful giver loves God, and loves him more deeply each time he gives.

Adapted from *Money, Possessions and Eternity* by Randy Alcorn © 1989. Used by permission of Tyndale House Publishers, Inc. All rights reserved.

SPIRITUAL EXERCISE

I
t's a bold statement: "Money and possessions are an index of your spiritual life." Certainly, Jesus did nothing to take the edge off. In fact, he reduced this truth to the simplest of terms when he said, "Where your treasure is, there your heart will be also" (Matt. 6:21).

Your assignment for this session is to engage in an exercise of ruthlessly honest observation concerning your heart and your treasures. This week, as you interact with money and possessions—as you make purchases, walk through stores, read magazines, watch TV, interact with peers, manage your household—ask yourself this question: *"What is going on in my heart right now?"*

Take specific note of these (or other) thoughts or feelings (or the lack of them!) related to money and possessions that are triggered throughout the day:

Delight	Dissatisfaction	Envy
Disappointment	Anxiety	Excitement
Insecurity	Peace of mind	Gratitude
Contentment	Guilt	Trust
Greed	Anger	Regret

At the end of each day, have a brief time of reflection. Make a few notes in your journal or another place. What are you seeing in yourself? Is there any dominant pattern? Anything that surprises you? What summary statements can you make?

> NOTE: We want to offer one important caution. It could be very easy during this exercise to slip into evaluating and criticizing yourself. "I shouldn't be feeling this." "I have to stop thinking that." That is not the point of this exercise. The purpose here is to help you see reality. If you move too quickly into self-criticism or immediate attempts to change, it will be harder to stay objective. And, at best, any changes will tend to be superficial. Your challenge for now—like that of a good reporter—is to engage in detached, nonjudgmental observation.

1. The reading states, "In a sense, how we relate to money and possessions is the story of our lives." Take a few moments to reflect on your upbringing. How would you summarize the story of your family's life concerning money and possessions as you were growing up?

What kind of training in money management, if any, did your parents give you, and what impact did it have?

What other perspectives about money did you catch from their attitudes and behaviors, positive or negative?

2. According to the reading, there is a sense in which our relationship to money "forms our biography." If someone were to read your biography—if they came to know you only by "reading" your attitudes and behaviors toward money and possessions—what five words would they use to describe you? (Consider asking a close friend to supplement your list.)

What truth does money tell about you that few people know?

3. Summarize the money-management principles found in Proverbs 6:6–11 and 27:23–27.

Now summarize Jesus' teaching in Matthew 6:25–34.

How do you resolve the differences between these apparently conflicting teachings of Scripture?

NOTE: Often in the Bible, we come across two or more strains of teaching that seem to be at odds. As we obey one command, we seem to be disobeying another. In our day, we sometimes advise, "Look before you leap" and then turn around and declare, "He who hesitates is lost." These proverbs seem to offer opposite counsel. But each addresses a human weakness which at some point needs correction. When we first know the audience and the circumstances, we can determine when to apply which saying. Like two sides of a coin, both statements are needful. It requires wisdom to make the appropriate application.

As we attempt to resolve the tension points in Scripture—and there are many when it comes to money and possessions—we must grapple with both sides of the coin. As we wrestle with our situation, listen to the Spirit, and seek godly counsel, we will be able to determine his application for us while preserving all aspects of what he commands in his Word.

4. Read 1 Timothy 6:6–10. Summarize the various principles taught in this passage.

What important point does Paul make in verse 10?

How have you seen the love of money at the root of some evil affecting your life? Be specific.

Do you think the solution is to *despise* money? Why or why not?

5. Read Acts 2:42–47 and 4:32–35. Although this was a unique period in history (the very beginning of the church), what do you believe are some timeless principles from these verses that apply to all Christians, even today?

6. What fears do you have about living more in line with the principles expressed in questions 3, 4, and 5? Are there any topics relating to good stewardship that you are dreading talking about in this study? Why?

7. We all know Judas as the one who betrayed Christ. What else do we learn about Judas from John 12:4–6 and Mark 14:10–11?

No one expected Judas to be the one who was going to defect. Yet clues to his true character were available—if anyone had bothered to look—in the ways he handled money. Comment on the link you see between how we manage our money and the condition of our souls.

8. How does your current handling of money make it clear that God is important to you? Be specific.

Describe how God's work in your life caused those practices to come about.

How does faith play a part in these habits?

9. More than almost any other area of our lives, our handling of money and possessions reveals what we believe—not what we *say* we believe, but what we *really* believe. What do your actual day-to-day patterns regarding money and possessions indicate that you really believe with respect to the following statements? On each continuum, place an X where you see yourself.

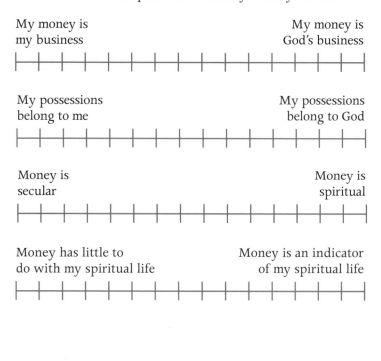

My money is
my business

My money is
God's business

My possessions
belong to me

My possessions
belong to God

Money is
secular

Money is
spiritual

Money has little to
do with my spiritual life

Money is an indicator
of my spiritual life

10. Where do you place yourself on the following continuum?

God is displeased with my
financial life

God is pleased with my
financial life

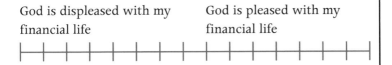

What do you want to see happen in your life through the course of this study? Give God an open invitation to do his work in your life.

TAKE-AWAY

My summary of the main point of this session, and how it impacts me personally:

> NOTE: You will fill in this information after your group discussion. Leave it blank until the conclusion of your meeting.

SESSION TWO

THE OPEN HANDS
OF GOD

The Open Hands of God

Reading adapted from a message by Bill Hybels

L ook at your hands. When you were just an infant, you came out with your hands closed. And every time somebody put their little finger by yours, you would wrap your hand around it, hold on tight, and not let go. As a toddler, you started grabbing rattles and little toys. When another kid came in your direction and wanted to take them away from you, you said, "Mine," and held on tight.

For most of us, clutching is like breathing. It just comes naturally.

When you were in junior high school, you hung on tightly to bicycle handlebars and batons and other things. In high school you hung on to the hand of Betty Lou, and you were not about to let that go. In college you hung on to a lot of different stuff—maybe some stuff we don't even want to talk about here—but when you left, you were clutching a diploma with two hands.

When you started a career, you grabbed the lowest rung on the ladder and you hung on. Then you reached for the second one and you hung on, and then the next one. Since then, you have been climbing ladders, clutching rungs. Someday retirement will come and you'll hang on to golf clubs or gardening tools, pension funds, and social security. When you get near the end of your life, you'll start hanging on to canes and walkers.

And then do you know what happens to some people in the final moments of their life? They clutch the edge of a hospital bed. They hang on tightly as if to life itself. And then they die. Finally, they relax their grip.

By nature, you and I are clutchers. We scrape and claw and work and fret, and if we get ahead just a little bit, we hold on. It doesn't matter who or what tries to convince us to relax our grip. We have a reflexive response when it comes to giving up something that's dear to us: "No way—not for him, not for her, not even for God."

For most of us, clutching is like breathing. It just comes naturally.

The Generosity of God

What a difference between our hands and the hands of God. In creation, God lavishly formed and fashioned. He created that which was good—very good. And then he opened up his hands. He gave his creation to those he created as a gift to be cared for and enjoyed.

When someone— anyone—comes to the point of reaching out to God, they can fully expect open hands from him.

Throughout the history of God's people, God opened his hands and generously provided them with food, drink, protection, blessing, and love. The psalmist declared, "You open your hand and satisfy the desires of every living thing" (Ps. 145:16). The prophet Jeremiah proclaimed, ". . . his compassions never fail. They are new every morning; great is your faithfulness" (Lam. 3:22–23). God's kindness and generosity are not fading. His inclination toward us is not changing. His resources are not drying up. Bound up in the very heart of God is the desire to shower his children with goodness.

When Jesus came and saw the needs of people, he opened *his* hands. He taught, healed, touched, loved, fed, and freed. And when he was about to be nailed to the cross as a sin payment for all of us, he did not hold on to his life. He did not shake a clenched fist at those nailing him to the cross. He opened his hands.

It is one of the most profound promises of Scripture. When someone—*anyone*—comes to the point of reaching out to God, they can fully expect open hands from him.

The open hands of God are merely the outward symbol of an inner reality—God's generosity. Generosity is that part of God that sincerely enjoys giving to others in a liberal manner, leaving recipients gasping and saying, "What a God. What an outlandishly generous God!" This is the lavishness that so distinguishes his hands from ours.

Look at your hands again. Just take a peek. Do you like what you see? Do you wish your hands looked a little bit more like the hands of Christ? Do you? Don't start wringing them and wrenching them. Leave them alone. Because if God needs to change your hands, he does not usually start there. If he needs to change your hands, he will likely start with your heart.

Changed Heart, Changed Hands

A pair of hands were transformed by Jesus one day. They were attached to a man named Zacchaeus. We don't know that much about him, but we do know that he was a clutcher. In fact, he didn't just have an iron grip on his own stuff, he also wrenched whatever he could from the hands of others.

If he needs to change your hands, he will likely start with your heart.

Zacchaeus was a clutcher . . . until he had dinner with Jesus. We are not given the details of what went on in that conversation, but Zacchaeus comes out the other side with transformed hands.

Here is what I imagine Jesus might have said over dinner: "Hey, Zacchaeus. What your heart yearns for will never be satisfied by that which you are hanging on to so tightly. Your heart was meant to be in deep communion with God and in loving community with other people in the Family of God. You have walked away from that kind of communion and are settling for something far less. You are settling for trying to meet the needs of your heart by clutching stuff."

I think Jesus might have gone on, "You know what I am going to do for you? In the not too distant future, I am going to open up my hands and they are going to receive steel spikes so that guys like you with hands like yours can be changed. I am going to be so generous to you, Zacchaeus. I am going to take your sin and greed and lack of love and I am going to pay for it on the cross and present salvation to you as a gift.

"And I won't stop there. I am going to adopt you into my family. I am going to answer your prayers. I am going to give you strength through the storms of life. And I am going to give you heaven on top of it all."

At a certain point in the conversation, I think the enormity of Jesus' generosity melted Zacchaeus and something changed on the inside. Zacchaeus emerges with his voice trembling with excitement and newfound conviction. "Here and now I give half of my possessions to the poor, and if I have cheated anybody out of anything, I will pay back four times the amount" (Luke 19:8).

When your heart gets transformed by generous grace, your hands have a way of opening up.

Ambushed by Love

When your heart gets transformed by generous grace, your hands have a way of opening up.

Some time ago, my college-aged daughter snuck into my office while I was out to lunch one day. She came in stealthy fashion and left Post-it notes all over my office—on my desk, under the phone console, on shelves of the bookcases, in my top desk drawer. For days afterward, I was still finding them hidden in places. The notes said things like, "I love you, Dad," "There has never been a little girl who loved her dad more," and so on.

I cannot describe the effect that her lavish act had on me. I sat in my office chair in a pile and just soaked it in. I felt it changing me. Her generous expressions of love confronted me everywhere I turned.

You are in a relationship with a God who does that kind of thing all the time. He paints the sky with a sunset and says, "I love you." He answers your prayers and says, "See, I love you." He strengthens you when you are weak and says, "I love you." He lavishly supplies daily provisions and says, "Remember, I love you." When you are in desperate need of grace, he opens his forgiving arms and says, "I love you."

God's generous expressions of love confront you everywhere you turn. The question is: Do you see them? Do you take the time to notice? Do you ever sit back in your chair and let the message of all his divine Post-it notes soak in?

Look at your hands one last time. What is the truth about them? One thing is certain. If you live deeply enough with a sense of God's generosity, your hands will start looking more like his. They really will. They will start opening up more frequently. They will start opening up to a wider range of needs. They will start staying open for longer periods of time.

And you will learn perhaps the most surprising thing of all. In the opening of your hands you will find what your clenched hands never could: joy. Real joy!

SPIRITUAL EXERCISE

I t's inconceivable that the dad would have been too busy or too preoccupied to notice his daughter's Post-it note barrage. And yet we routinely rush past the daily reminders God gives us of his generosity.

This week, your challenge is to *notice*. Slow yourself. Open your eyes. Observe God's generosity to *you*. Be on the lookout for the ways, large and small, that he opens his hands to you. Pay close attention to details.

- Notice God's material generosity that you tend to take for granted—a warm bed, a closet full of clothes, a hot shower, a good meal.
- Observe the physical blessings that most of us enjoy—the ability to see, hear, walk, think.
- Pay attention to wholesome pleasures that bring you joy, specific answers to prayer, scenes of natural beauty that refresh you.
- Recognize God's grace expressed through a loving friend or the richness of his people gathered for worship.

One way to carry out this exercise is to literally carry a pad of Post-it notes with you. Every time you become aware of something God has done or has given you, jot it down on a note. At the end of each day, have a central location (the refrigerator door, the back of your office door, a mirror) where you place the notes. (If you choose not to use the notes, then keep a running list.)

How does this exercise change the way you view God? If the notes are on your mirror, what is it like to have a hard time seeing yourself because of all the blessings that are getting "in the way"? Do you sense any connection between the open hands of God to you and the posture of your hands toward others?

Be prepared to share some of your observations at the next small group meeting.

BIBLE STUDY

1. Describe a time when someone overwhelmed you with an act of lavish generosity. What touched you most deeply about that act?

   What, if any, long-term impact did that have on you?

   Based on that experience, what statement would you make about the power of generosity?

2. King David lived with a keen awareness of the generosity of his God. Psalm 65 is just one of David's many writings that recollect the Post-it note barrage of God's kindness. Read the entire psalm a few times, then itemize every way in which God lavishly opened his hands to David and the people of Israel.

What blessings especially stand out for you?

If you were writing that psalm, is there anything you would have added to the list?

3. Sometimes we think that God's gifts are only "spiritual" in nature. But God is the author of enjoyment, including the enjoyment of material blessings. Read Deuteronomy 14:22–26 and 16:13–15. What does God instruct his people to do as a part of these festivals?

In what way do these instructions surprise you?

How do you react to the fact that God not only allowed but *mandated* these times of celebration—and even used a portion of the people's tithe to underwrite them? How does this challenge your view of God?

4. Consider these words of Dallas Willard, from his book *The Spirit of the Disciplines:* "How many people are radically and permanently repelled from The Way by Christians who are unfeeling, stiff, unapproachable, boringly lifeless, obsessive, and dissatisfied? Yet such Christians are everywhere, and what they are missing is the wholesome liveliness springing from a balanced vitality within the freedom of God's loving rule."

Why is it so important that any concept of good stewardship be firmly rooted in the generosity of God and a grateful embrace of his wholesome pleasures?

5. Read 2 Corinthians 8:9 and Philippians 2:5–11. In both cases, Christ opened his hands and let go of something he had every right to grasp. Describe what it was that Christ let go of.

What were the results of Christ's choices?

What would your life be like today if Jesus had chosen to grasp instead of release?

6. Now consider the posture of your own hands, particularly with respect to money and possessions. Reflect on the past week or so. Were there specific instances when you felt your hands instinctively clutching—times when you wanted to retain, withhold, assert your rights, or protect your turf? Describe those moments.

What factors contributed to this tendency? (Fear? Anger? Greed? Envy?)

Were there any instances when you specifically fought the urge to grasp, and were openhanded instead? Describe.

Overall, would an objective person say that you are more generous with respect to your money and possessions than you were a year ago, or less so?

7. Consider again this statement: "More than almost any other area of our life, our handling of money and possessions reveals what we believe—not what we *say* we believe, but what we *really* believe." Being as candid as possible, what would you say you really believe concerning the faithful generosity of God?

Is this belief reflected in your trend line (in question 6)? If not, how do you account for the difference?

My summary of the main point of this session, and how it impacts me personally:

NOTE: You will fill in this information after your group discussion. Leave it blank until the conclusion of your meeting.

Tithing: A Training Exercise for the Heart

Reading by John Ortberg and Laurie Pederson

More.

These four letters constitute one of the most powerful words in the English language. Very smart people stay up at night trying to figure out ways to convince us that we are (or ought to be) discontent, and that we would experience true satisfaction if we just had *more.*

All day long we are bombarded by the prophets of more. *Use me, buy me, drive me, wear me, try me, put me in your hair.* The things we can obtain just for more hair satisfaction are staggering! You can wash it, blow-dry it, condition it, color it, straighten it if it's too curly, curl it if it's too straight, wax it if it grows where it shouldn't, or Rogain it if it doesn't grow where it should. Just a little more of someone's product and your hair is sure to be happy.

More is an insatiable desire and, unfortunately, not limited to something as trivial as hair. Serving the "more monster" can never satisfy our souls. Yet in the short run, saying no to "more" can be difficult, even frightening.

No one sets out to be a greedy person, but it happens all the time—even in the church. Jesus saw it becoming an issue and made this sobering statement: "No one can serve two masters; for a slave will either hate the one and love the other, or be devoted to the one and despise the other. You cannot serve God and wealth" (Matt. 6:24 NRSV). Jesus didn't say this to be harsh. He was just stating

Serving the "more monster" can never satisfy our souls.

things the way they are. There is not room for two masters in a single human heart.

What does it take to tame the monster of more? What does it take to transform a heart from greed to generosity? For most of us, it will not come simply by acquiring more knowledge, applying more willpower, or even by studying more Scripture, as important as those things are. The more monster is too strong. We need a way of training. We need a tangible and routine way to say, "Sorry, money, you are not on the throne. You will not be the god of my life today."

What we need, God has provided. It's called *tithing*.

The Heart of the Tithe

What just came to your mind as you read the word *tithing*? A mechanical obligation? A religious tax? A fund-raising mechanism? An impossible requirement?

What just came to your mind as you read the word tithing? *A mechanical obligation? A religious tax? A fund-raising mechanism? An impossible requirement?*

We need to begin in the Old Testament to see just what God had in mind when he invented tithing:

A tithe of everything from the land, whether grain from the soil or fruit from the trees, belongs to the LORD; it is holy to the LORD.

—Leviticus 27:30

The literal meaning of the word *tithe* is "a tenth part." People tend to use the word loosely today. They may speak of tithing ten dollars a week when their income is $50,000 per year. For the math-impaired among us, giving ten dollars a week would be tithing only if my income were $100 a week. The Israelites were raised on the practice of tithing. To them, tithing clearly meant giving ten percent, not two percent or four percent.

Strategically linked to the concept of the tithe was the concept of firstfruits.

Honor the LORD with your wealth, with the firstfruits of all your crops.

—Proverbs 3:9

Firstfruit giving was a concept that largely overlapped with tithing—and probably referred to the same gifts. But where tithing stressed the exact amount, the giving of firstfruits emphasized a spiritual principle: God is the Giver of the harvest. All we have is a gift from God, and we want to honor him with the first and best that we've received. For Israel, the first and the best of the wheat harvested, the first and best of the wool sheared, the first and best of the fruit gathered all belonged to God. The message of firstfruits was not complex: God deserves better than leftovers.

Firstfruit tithing is one of the richest spiritual practices in all of Scripture. It provides a powerful series of reminders built into the very rhythm of our lives.

Every time I tithe, I remind myself that God is on the throne. Not me. Not money.

Every time I tithe, I reinforce that all I have is from him. The tithe is not a tip for good service, as though God were some helper I could patronize. He is the Owner, I am the steward.

Every time I tithe, I make a declaration: "I will trust you, God"—even when trusting doesn't feel easy or natural.

Every time I tithe, I am reminded, even as I calculate the amount of my check, of how much I've been given. I count my blessings, and in doing so, I put to death (or at least injure) the more monster in me.

There is an unmistakable connection in Scripture between tithing and spiritual life itself. Israel's giving patterns were a consistent thermometer of the nation's inner spiritual condition.

When the Israelites' hearts were kindled with a spirit of worship to God, they overflowed with contagious expressions of generosity—freewill offerings exceeding any tithe. So great was their giving that on one occasion, it actually got out of hand and had to be restrained! (Ex. 36:5–7). Can you imagine the police being called in these days to control an outburst of uncontrolled giving?

God deserves better than leftovers.

But when Israel's hearts turned to ingratitude, complaint, and idolatry, their hands withheld. And the more their hands withheld, the more their hearts turned away from God. As their hearts went, so went their giving. As their giving went, so went their hearts.

A Floor, Not a Ceiling

Some people argue that since tithing is found in the Old Testament, we can discard the whole concept. But Jesus is clear. He did not come to *abolish* the law. He came to *fulfill* it (Matt. 5:17). He came to bring the law to its perfect conclusion through grace.

Grace was a reality that penetrated the heart of everyone in the infant church. And it was grace-filled hearts that led once again to open hands.

"The tithe was not a ceiling, it was merely a floor."

> *... there was complete agreement of heart and soul. Not one of them claimed any of his possessions as his own but everything was common property ... and a wonderful spirit of generosity pervaded the whole fellowship. Indeed, there was not a single person in need among them.*
>
> —Acts 4:32–34 PHILLIPS

In that generosity-infused environment, it's impossible to imagine anyone saying, "Thank goodness grace takes us out from under the law. Now we don't have to tithe any more. We can give far less than ten percent and keep the rest for ourselves!"

In the words of Randy Alcorn, "The tithe was not a ceiling, it was merely a floor." It was a beginning point from which Christ-followers gave much more as needs arose.

A Time to Test God

> *"Bring the whole tithe into the storehouse, that there may be food in my house. Test me in this," says the* LORD *Almighty, "and see if I will not throw open the floodgates of heaven and pour out so much blessing that you will not have room enough for it."*
>
> —Malachi 3:10

"Test me in this," God said. This is the only time in Scripture when you are invited—no, *urged*—to test the goodness of God.

Will you? If you do, God promises two things in return: blessings on earth and treasures forever in heaven. Who could ask for *more*?

I t is more blessed to give than to receive" (Acts 20:35). This phrase certainly has to be in the running for the most-quoted-words-of-Jesus award. The question is, do you really believe it? It is easy to mouth agreement with this principle, to say it is true. But our actual giving patterns tell the truth about what we really believe. This week, sit down and take a look back through your financial records (checkbook, credit card statements, etc.) for the past month or two. Then answer the following questions:

- Did anything surprise you, good or bad, as you did this review?

- Was there any cringe factor? Were there any evidences of the "more monster" rearing its head?

- Did you tithe? Did you actually give one-tenth of your earnings to God as soon as you received them?

- If you didn't actually tithe, what percentage did you give to God? Is that percentage higher or lower than last year? Than five years ago?

- Were there any spontaneous outbursts of generosity—modest or even substantial sacrifices made for the sake of someone in need?

- Did any expenditures represent a step of faith?

Now answer the question again. "Do I *really* believe it is more blessed to give than to receive?"

BIBLE STUDY

1. The hunger for more is not a twentieth- or twenty-first-century phenomenon. It's as old as the garden of Eden. Unfortunately, God's people have been anything but immune to this appetite. Psalm 106 reviews Israel's history during the days of the Exodus from Egypt. How does the theme of wanting more come through in this passage?

   What were the results?

   When the hunger for more happens in your life, what form does it usually take? In what areas are you most vulnerable? (House? Car? Recreation? Clothing?)

2. Read Jesus' words in Matthew 6:19–24, then paraphrase them below.

Do you really think it's impossible to serve two masters? Why?

In what ways have you tried to do so? Be specific.

3. Suppose you decided today to stop wanting more and to forever cease the tendency to serve money and possessions. What would you do to achieve that resolution?

How successful do you think willpower and effort alone would be?

Spiritual disciplines are those practices or experiences that train you to do ultimately what you cannot do today, even by trying really hard. In what way do you think God intends tithing to be a spiritual discipline to help us train our hearts away from materialistic tendancies?

NOTE: The Israelites actually had three tithes. The first supported their spiritual leaders, the Levites (Num. 18:21, 24). The second was used for a feast (Deut. 14:22–23). The third, taken every three years, was for the poor (Deut. 14:28–29). On top of this were other voluntary offerings. The cumulative effect was a minimal annual sharing of more than 23 percent of a person's gross income. Against that backdrop, the simple tithe (10 percent) looks even more modest as a baseline for giving.

4. Sometimes we forget that God has feelings too. In the final book of the Old Testament, Malachi, we get a glimpse of God's strong feelings in response to the giving patterns of his people. Review Malachi 1:6–14 and 3:8–12. What were the offenses of God's people?

Why do you think this was (and is) so hurtful to God?

As expressed in the reading, God does not threaten to punish Israel's disobedience. Instead, he offers them a test—a test of him. Paraphrase God's challenge (Mal. 3:10).

What do you think is God's timeless teaching—his message to you—based on these passages?

5. In 1 Chronicles 29, we read how David and others provided materials for the building of the temple. Read verses 1–20, then comment on the following:

The heart behind his giving.

The impact of his giving on those around him.

What David *really* believed.

6. How do you respond to the statement in the reading that the tithe was never meant to be a ceiling, only a floor?

How do Paul's words in 2 Corinthians 9:6–12 support that statement?

7. Reflect on the following two statements and comment on how you think they are true in your life:

Giving *reveals* your heart.

Giving *shapes* your heart.

As a result of this study, what is being revealed about your heart—positive or negative? Is there anything you sense God pointing out to you?

What additional heart-shaping do you think he wants to accomplish in you specifically through the spiritual discipline of tithing?

TAKE-AWAY

My summary of the main point of this session, and how it impacts me personally:

> NOTE: You will fill in this information after your group discussion. Leave it blank until the conclusion of your meeting.

SESSION FOUR

BEHIND THE SCENES OF DEBT

Behind the Scenes of Debt

Reading adapted from a message by Bill Hybels

I f someone were to ask you to list the most powerful forces at work in your life, what would you say? Perhaps you would think of the power of love, the power of hope, the power of a dream, the power of community. When was the last time you thought of the amazing power of *interest*? Very few people would think to put interest anywhere near their top ten. But maybe they should.

Debt can undermine the power of love. It can destroy the power of hope.

One Sunday morning after I gave a message on this subject, a guy stopped to talk to me. He had racked up a debt of $7,500 on his credit cards. "But that stops today," he said. "I'm going to figure out what the minimum monthly payment is, and I'm going to pay it until it's all paid."

I prayed with him, encouraged him, and said, "Go for it."

Afterward, I did a little figuring. If that guy did not add a single dollar more to his debt, and if he diligently made the minimum payments until the debt was removed, how long do you think it would take him to pay off that debt? If you guessed 30 years and 2 months, you'd be right. And how much will he have paid to get rid of that $7,500 debt? *$23,000!*

Debt can undermine the power of love. It can destroy the power of hope. It can dash the power of a dream. It can divide community. Get on the wrong side of interest and it can destroy your life.

Why Say No to Debt

In our heart of hearts, most of us know that debt is not a good thing. Certainly, Scripture is clear. "The borrower is servant to the lender," says Proverbs 22:7.

J. Rubin Clark puts it this way: "Once you're in debt, interest will be your companion every minute of the day or night, and it's working against you. It has no love, no sympathy. It is as hard and soulless as a granite cliff, and you cannot dismiss it. Whenever you get in its way or you cross its course or fail to meet its demands, it crushes you." Maybe you know this all too well.

Every time you sign up for any kind of debt, you're surrendering a huge piece of freedom. You're giving it to someone else who is going to be a taskmaster. The lender says "jump" and you say "how high?"

Debt has an uncanny way of unmasking our character flaws.

Debt obligates you to earning pressures. When you're nostril deep in debt, any ripple of disruption to your income stream is life-threatening. These days, one income stream is rarely enough to keep abreast of the payments. You'd better have two jobs and never miss a day of work. The mere mention of layoffs keeps you living in constant panic. There's not a lot of freedom in that.

Debt undermines joy. How do you really enjoy a dinner out with your family or friends or a weekend away when you're deep in debt? Somewhere deep in your conscience, you say to yourself, "We shouldn't be doing this. We shouldn't be buying that. Not in the financial condition we're in." It robs your joy.

Debt erodes giving opportunities. When you're deep in debt, and a wonderful giving opportunity comes along—the chance to help a loved one, the poor, the cause of Christ in the world—your heart says, "I'd love to do that." But your wallet says, "It's not there to give." It's a huge tension for a Christ-follower to have a heart overflowing with compassion but a financial statement overflowing with debt.

There's one more downside to debt. Sooner or later, deeply indebted people are forced to look in the mirror and see the face that put them into debt. It's hard to admit, but debt has an uncanny way of unmasking our character flaws—a mysterious habit of exposing those areas that we'd just as soon leave in the darkness, but that most need to be brought into the light.

A Contentment Deficit?

If you take that long look in the mirror, you might find that what makes you so debt-prone is a basic lack of contentment. Hebrews 13:5 says, "Keep your lives free from the love of money and be content with what you have."

Are you content? Some of us have never grown in this aspect of spiritual life. We have never learned how to say: *Enough. I have enough. I can get along without that. I don't really need a new one of those.*

So much of our discontentment stems from an inability to distinguish between wants and needs. Of course, Madison Avenue works overtime to ensure that the line stays blurry.

So much of our discontentment stems from an inability to distinguish between wants and needs.

My parents gave me a great gift in this regard. Whenever I would say, "Dad, I need a new bike," or "I need a new baseball glove," I can still hear him reply: "Billy, there's a huge difference between wants and needs. You don't *need* a new bike. You don't need a baseball glove, although you may want it. I'll tell you what you need. You need air, food, and a little water. That's what you *need*. Pretty much everything else is in the *want* category. So keep that straight."

There's nothing wrong with identifying some things that are in the want category. God is infinitely generous with his children. Paul affirmed in 1 Timothy 6:17 that God "richly provides us with everything for our enjoyment." He actually likes seeing us enjoy some material pleasures.

But when those wants lead us down the path of indebtedness, when they take away money that should be going to God or that we should be saving, then we have a problem.

Racing Ahead of God

Much indebtedness reveals a lack of patience. When you really want something, you have to have it *now*. If you look one layer beneath the impatience, often what you'll find is a basic lack of trust in God's goodness.

There is a passage I stumbled on many years ago. It's 2 Samuel 12:7–8. David had just committed the terrible sin of adultery with Bathsheba. The prophet Nathan comes to speak the corrective words of God to David.

> *This is what the LORD, the God of Israel says: "I anointed you king over Israel, and I delivered you from the hand of Saul. I gave your master's house to you. . . . I gave you the house of Israel and Judah. And if all this had been too little, I would have given you even more. Why did you despise the word of the LORD by doing what is evil in his eyes?"*

I would have given you even more.

I watch the same television you watch. I'm tempted by the same stuff you're tempted by all the time. There are some things that I look at and I want them so badly. And I know I could just sign up for a loan to get them. I could just pull out the credit card. But I keep reflecting on the message of God to David, "I would have given you more if you would have waited and obeyed."

Some of us just have to trust the goodness of God. If we wait, he'll be gracious. If we wait, he will provide. If we wait, he will satisfy us with the best possible gifts. We don't have to run out ahead of him. In fact, we'll be in trouble if we do.

What would your credit card balance say about your patience and trust in God's goodness these days? Are you racing ahead of God?

Thou Shalt Not Compete with the Joneses

If you take a courageous look in the mirror, perhaps you would have to admit that your greatest area of difficulty is with the tenth commandment—"Thou shalt not covet." Or in today's vernacular, "Thou shalt not compete with the Joneses."

What is coveting? It's looking at your neighbor's stuff and instead of simply appreciating it or being happy for them because they have it, it's saying, "I've got to get me one of those." Whatever somebody else has, you want.

There's only one way out of this competitive madness. Declare your neighbor the winner! Just say, "Take the victory lap. You win. You win the car game, the house game, the landscape game, the Christmas light contest. Your snowblower is bigger. You win!"

Have you ever asked yourself what the neighborhood winner really gets for beating all the other Joneses? A heart full of anxiety and a wheelbarrow full of debt. It's a shallow victory, and short-lived too!

What is it for you? When you take a long look in the mirror, what pulls you to possess what you cannot pay for? In the final analysis, might it be that your debt is less a financial issue and more of a spiritual one?

Fight to Stay Free

There is one debt you will never be able to repay, no matter how long you work or how hard you try. The principal balance is just too high. That is the debt you owe God. But there is a cross. And there is a Savior. And he says, "Your debt is cancelled. Your account is wiped clean, simply because I love you."

Christ paid a costly price to purchase your freedom. Don't give it back to the bondage of indebtedness. Don't become the lender's slave. Fight to stay free!

There is one debt that you will never be able to repay, no matter how long you work or how hard you try. That is the debt you owe God.

SPIRITUAL EXERCISE

The reading identified various character flaws that underlie debt (they are summarized below). Which of these had the biggest "ouch" factor for you?

Now consider these key verses that apply to each trait:

Character Weaknesses	Scripture
Lack of contentment	"Keep your lives free from the love of money and be content with what you have ..." (Heb. 13:5).
Confusing wants and needs	"But if we have food and clothing, we will be content with that" (1 Tim. 6:8).
Getting ahead of God through impatience and failing to trust him	"Put [your] hope in God, who richly provides us with everything for our enjoyment" (1 Tim. 6:17).
Covetousness	"Let no debt remain outstanding, except the continuing debt to love one another. ... Do not covet" (Rom. 13:8–9).

You may think of other verses that apply to your particular weakness. Consider writing those out to help you.

Having identified your specific weakness and the scriptural "antidote," start each day bringing to mind the verse from God's Word that applies to your situation. Do it as early as possible, maybe even while you're still lying in bed. When you end your day, again remind yourself of God's truth.

Here's the biggest challenge: as you go through your day, every time you make a purchase, call this verse to mind. Consider postponing *every* discretionary purchase you make this week by at least twenty-four hours. Tell yourself that if you still think it's a good idea, you'll buy it tomorrow. If not, you've saved yourself from another impulse purchase.

What happens as you walk away from these purchases? How do you feel when you come back after a twenty-four-hour cooldown period? Do you ever regret waiting? Be prepared to share the results of your experience at the next group meeting.

1. Proverbs 22:7 is a bedrock verse concerning avoidance of debt. But what really happens when you're a slave to a lender? Jot down five words or short phrases that describe the slavery into which debt forces you.

NOTE: Some debt is caused by accidents, injury, or emergencies that are unavoidable. But that is not the kind of debt that most of us carry. Most Christian financial advisors would say that there's only one kind of debt that you ever ought to consider seriously, and that's the debt of an appreciating item—a reasonable home mortgage or a well-thought-out business loan where prayerful and discerning people would agree it is an appreciating situation. All other debts should be avoided.

---

2. Near Proverbs 22:7 are several other verses that shed light on character issues often related to indebtedness. After each passage, describe the possible connection between its teaching and a debt-plagued person.

Proverbs 22:3

Proverbs 22:4

Proverbs 22:9

Proverbs 22:26–27

Proverbs 23:1–3

Proverbs 23:4–5

Which of the above speaks most to you? Why?

3. The reading pointed out four main character issues that contribute to debt. The first was contentment. Think of a situation when you struggled with contentment. What do you think was at the root of your discontentment?

Paul spoke of how he'd mastered discontentment in Philippians 4:12. Part of how he learned this skill is revealed in verse 13. What is the essence of that teaching?

What additional insights are contained in the following verses from chapter 4 as to how Paul maintained his level of contentment?

v. 4

v. 6

v. 8

v. 19

4. A closely related character issue is confusing *wants* and *needs*. Paul lays out the basics of this issue in 1 Timothy 6:8. On either side of that verse, he gives some helpful teaching about what causes that confusion. What factors does he identify in verses 9–10?

He makes a profound point in verses 6–7. How might this help you in your attempts to differentiate between a need and want?

5. The next character issues discussed in the reading were getting ahead of God through impatience and failure to trust him. Sum up Jesus' teaching as it relates to this issue in Matthew 6:25–33.

Paul's words in Romans 8:31–32 also touch on this issue. Why do you think it's sometimes hard to believe—to really trust—what Paul says is true of God?

How have you been struggling with financial patience lately? (What would your credit card reveal?)

6. The last area covered in the reading was covetousness. According to James 4:1–3, to what can covetousness lead?

Verse 2 says we should ask God for what we want instead of coveting. What's your reaction to that advice?

Verse 3 makes it clear that it might not be as simple as asking God. What else is necessary?

Seeing something often increases the desire to possess it. What would probably decrease the desire? What do you need to do to stop frequently seeing the things you covet?

7. How much debt do you currently have? Be specific and comprehensive.

What character issues must you work on to avoid this kind of debt in the future?

What is your plan to get out of debt? In what ways can those in your small group help you?

Note: Those who counsel people in debt advise a three-step solution:

1. **RESOLVE:** Make a resolute decision today to get free of debt
2. **PLAN:** Create a written plan for complete debt retirement
3. **PARTNER:** Get others involved as accountability partners and encouragers

If you are struggling in this area, get someone to help you. There are many good Christian counselors and programs that can provide tangible assistance. You really can be free from this tyranny, and it will be worth whatever price you pay to get there!

TAKE-AWAY

My summary of the main point of this session, and how it impacts me personally:

NOTE: You will fill in this information after your group discussion. Leave it blank until the conclusion of your meeting.

SESSION
FIVE

What Is a Biblical Lifestyle?

Reading adapted from *Money, Possessions and Eternity* by Randy Alcorn

At times I crave an audible voice from heaven telling me exactly what I'm supposed to do with my money and possessions. Do you know the feeling? Philip Yancey perfectly expresses my dilemma when it comes to money:

Does grace mean I can freely pursue money and possessions to my heart's content? Or are money and possessions the root of all evil? How do we get clarity?

> *I feel pulled in opposite directions over the money issue. Sometimes I want to sell all that I own, join a Christian commune, and live out my days in intentional poverty. At other times, I want to rid myself of guilt and enjoy the fruits of our nation's prosperity. Mostly, I wish I did not have to think about money at all.*

Certainly, God gives us principles in his Word. Yet we are still left with a lot of latitude, which raises a lot of questions. In light of global needs, what should I possess? Should I own a house? A car? Two cars? If so, what kind of house and car? How many pairs of shoes is too many? Should I take a vacation that costs two hundred dollars but not one that costs two thousand?

Does grace mean I can freely pursue money and possessions to my heart's content? Or are money and possessions the root of all evil? How do we get clarity?

Materialism

There are two equally incorrect beliefs about money. The first is that money is automatically good. This is the belief of materialism. Webster's *New College Dictionary* defines materialism as "a theory that physical matter is the only or fundamental reality . . . that the highest values or objectives lie in material well-being. . . ."

Materialism begins with what we believe. Not merely what we say we believe, but the philosophy of life we actually live by. Hence, while any true Christian would deny belief in the philosophical underpinnings of materialism (he couldn't be a Christian if he didn't) he may nonetheless be preoccupied with material rather than spiritual things and therefore in fact be a practicing materialist.

Practicing materialists may say whatever they wish about the spiritual realm. They may go to church every week, serve communion or preach, but if they center their lives around the accumulation of things, they are, despite their most heated denials, materialists.

Materialism usually surfaces in one's lifestyle, but it is first and foremost a matter of the heart.

As the first man and woman valued what they considered appealing over what God said was right, so the materialist attaches the wrong price tags to things of this world as compared to the things of God. Of course, one need not actually buy or own an item to overvalue it. A materialist may be rich or poor, own much or own little, be a miser or a spendthrift. Materialism usually surfaces in one's lifestyle, but it is first and foremost a matter of the heart.

Examples of materialism fill the pages of Scripture and Jesus Christ sounded a sober warning against it: "Watch out! Be on your guard against all kinds of greed; a man's life does not consist in the abundance of his possessions" (Luke 12:15).

Materialism surfaces in two primary ways—possessiveness and covetousness. Possessiveness relates to what we have, covetousness to what we want. To be possessive is to be selfish and unsharing with what we own. To covet is to long for and to be preoccupied with having what God has not given us. It is the passion to possess what is not ours to have.

No matter how we may dislike the word "materialism," it perfectly describes the predominant mind-set of our society. It is not a harmless pastime, but a serious offense against God. Just as the lustful man is an adulterer (Matt. 5:28) and the hateful man a murderer (1 John 3:15), so the greedy man is an idolater (Col.3:5). Money-worship is a violation of the first and most fundamental of the Ten Commandments: "I am the LORD your God. . . . You shall have no other gods before me" (Ex. 20:2–3).

Jesus reinforced the point by telling the story of the rich fool (Luke 12:16–21). A fool is one who either does not recognize the truth or chooses to ignore it. The rich fool of the parable, building ever-bigger barns, thought he was a captain of his fate. He made his plans without taking into account God's plan. He failed to come to grips with three facts—the mortality of the present life, the eternality of the future life, and the fact that the future life is being forged by the present life. Though he probably believed there was a God, the rich fool was a fool precisely because he lived as if there were no God.

Materialism is not only wrong, it is terribly stupid.

"We brought nothing into the world, and we can take nothing out of it" (1 Tim. 6:7). You cannot take it with you. Materialism is not only wrong, it is terribly stupid.

So Should We Give Up Everything?

Materialism is money-centered and thing-centered rather than God-centered. It has no place in the Christian life. But is there an opposite extreme? I believe the answer is yes. It is asceticism.

An ascetic practices strict self-denial, depriving himself of all but the essential basics of the material world. Often asceticism is rooted in the philosophy of dualism, a belief that the spiritual world is good, but the physical world is evil.

By avoiding physical pleasures and conveniences, an ascetic thinks he is avoiding sin. The less you own, the more spiritual you are. If something isn't strictly essential, you shouldn't have it. But is this view truly the viewpoint of Scripture?

The entire fabric of Old Testament teaching argues against asceticism. The Jews did not labor under the notion that the physical world was bad and that God was not in it. On the contrary, they saw material things as from the hand of God, a Father's loving supply for his children. He was the Lord of the harvest, the Lord of life. As his grateful children, they celebrated at national feasts to rejoice in his material provisions, and in the process— frivolous as it may sound—had a great deal of fun.

Despite his serious mission, Jesus was often the prime host and guest of the party. And Paul, calling the ascetics of his day "hypocrites and liars," soundly declared, "Everything God created is good, and nothing is to be rejected . . ." (1 Tim. 4:4–5).

Martin Luther compared humanity to a drunkard who falls off his horse to the right, only to get back on and fall off to the left. In the matter of money and possessions, asceticism is falling off the horse one way, materialism the other. Satan cares little which side of the horse we fall off. He cares only that we don't stay in the saddle.

In the matter of money and possessions, asceticism is falling off the horse one way, materialism the other.

Choosing a Strategic Lifestyle

But seek first his kingdom and righteousness, and all these things will be given to you as well.

—Matthew 6:33

During World War II, when fuel was precious, billboards routinely asked motorists, "Is this trip necessary?" Every resource used for individual convenience was one less resource for the country's central concern, winning the war.

As Christians, we are also engaged in a great battle that requires great resources. We too must realize that spending resources on our own private concerns leaves less resources for our kingdom's central concern. We should ask, "Is this thing necessary?" Does this thing really contribute to my purpose in being here on this earth? Is this thing an asset to me as a soldier of Christ, or is it a liability? Ralph Winter uses the term "wartime lifestyle" to describe this strategic way of thinking.

If I am devoted to ascetic living, I might reject owning a computer because it is modern and nonessential. But if I live a wartime lifestyle, then the computer may serve as a strategic tool for kingdom purposes. Likewise, a microwave oven might be a luxury in one case but a useful tool in another, facilitating and freeing time to engage in the cause for which we are fighting. *Strategic living is always kingdom centered.*

Of course, the wartime mentality can be taken to such an extreme that we feel it is unfaithful to enjoy any possessions or special activities. This is not my perspective. Even in wartime, it is important to have a break from the battle. Soldiers need their rest and recreation. Life is not just utilitarian. There is nothing necessarily wrong with spending some money for modest pleasures that renew and revive us, especially since our battle is a lifetime in duration.

But if I have a strategic mentality, then I don't look at an increase in income simply as an opportunity to spend more but an opportunity to invest more in the cause. I might determine that I will live on a certain amount of money each year, allowing some room for discretionary or recreational spending. All income beyond that I will give to God's kingdom purposes. If he provides twice that basic amount of money I have designated for my living expense, then I will be giving away 50 percent of my income. If he provides four times that much, I will be giving away 75 percent of it.

All Christ's disciples are called to use their money and possessions to further the kingdom cause.

A Different View of Reality

Do such proposals seem strange? Have we forgotten that all Christ's disciples are called to use their money and possessions to further the kingdom cause? Have our peacetime lifestyles left us comfortable and complacent, unfit for battle and oblivious to the battle's eternal stakes?

In the words of Peter H. Davids, "A biblical lifestyle will necessarily recognize itself as being in opposition to the prevailing values and lifestyle of its culture. *It is informed by a different view of reality.*" This view of reality is not a harsh or austere view. It need not lead to bare-bones living, or to condemnation of those Christians who have greater opportunity or feel greater liberty to possess more than I do. Rather, it is a view toward the riches of the eternal kingdom.

Those who hold such a view are sincerely grateful for the refreshing pleasures and helpful possessions of this life. But regardless of what material things surround it, this view of reality remains focused on what is truly the greatest pleasure and possession of life, both here and hereafter—the pleasure of possessing Christ. It focuses on the knowledge that this world is not my home, and that while I'm here, my Lord is preparing for me my true home, and preparing me for it.

Adapted from *Money, Possessions and Eternity* by Randy Alcorn © 1989. Used by permission of Tyndale House Publishers, Inc. All rights reserved.

PURSUING SPIRITUAL TRANSFORMATION

A focal point. That is something we acutely need in order to negotiate the maze of choices and all the tugs—both internal and external—concerning money and possessions. In his book *Celebration of Discipline*, Richard Foster suggests,

> *Inwardly modern man is fractured and fragmented. He is trapped in a maze of competing attachments. One moment he makes decisions on the basis of sound reason and the next moment out of fear of what others will think of him. He has no unity or focus around which life is oriented.*

Such a focal point is just what Jesus provides in Matthew 6:33 when he says, "But seek first his kingdom and his righteousness, and all these things will be given to you as well."

The importance of Jesus' words cannot be overstated. According to him, *everything* hinges on putting the first things first.

What would this week look like if you really sought first God's kingdom and righteousness—particularly concerning your money and possessions? Memorize Jesus' words from Matthew 6:33. Punctuate your day with them. As you contemplate purchases, financial decisions, or lifestyle choices, stop and ask, "How can I seek first his kingdom and his righteousness right now in this choice?"

If the answer isn't immediately clear (and often it won't be), consider waiting before acting, if possible. Invite a few trusted believers into the conversation. Pray about it. Let Scripture speak to you. Seek the Spirit's guidance.

NOTE: Some of us are wired up to think that seeking God's kingdom always means saying no to things that bring us pleasure or joy. Others of us, if we're honest, lean to the other extreme, easily rationalizing a materialistic bent. It's important to be aware of your inclination and to avoid defaulting to it at each decision point. Seeking honest feedback in community can serve us well in this regard.

---

1. To what degree do you relate to the dilemma expressed early in the reading concerning lifestyle choices? When do you most feel the tension? How have you managed that tension in the past?

2. "What is God calling me to do?" is the key question for any believer wrestling with matters of lifestyle. With that in mind, take a few moments to review some of the specific "calls" that Jesus gave. After reading each passage, summarize the nature of the call and the lifestyle implications of each.

   Mark 1:16–20

   Mark 8:34–35

   Mark 10:17–22

   Mark 10:28

   Luke 14:33

   Based on these passages, what would you conclude any believer must do if he or she truly claims to be a Christ-follower?

3. It seems clear that true disciples must give up everything—
walk away from their homes, their money, and their possessions—if they want to truly follow Christ. Or do they? Based
on the following passages, what conclusion would you come to?

Luke 19:1–9

John 12:1–7

Acts 28:7–10

1 Timothy 6:17–19

It is apparent that these individuals did not abandon all their
possessions to serve Christ. But, in every case, what did they
do? How did they live out Christ's command to "give up"
everything?

How does that fit with the concept of strategic living discussed
in the reading? What do you think it means for you?

4. The very fact that the door is open to some legitimate differences in lifestyle leaves us open to a few traps. One is comparison. Being honest, how often are your choices made with one eye (and sometimes both!) focused on what other Christians around you are doing?

Do your comparisons usually lead you to live more frugally and with greater generosity, or do they usually give you permission to spend more and own more?

5. When we're not busy comparing, we're often busy judging. Christians are especially good at drawing a circle around our own lifestyle choices and labeling them "right," while looking critically at those who live differently. Describe the last time you engaged in that kind of thinking. Were you critical because someone lived more lavishly than you or less so?

Read John 21:20–22. While Jesus' response to Peter did not specifically involve a financial lifestyle issue, his words nevertheless confront the tendency to compare and judge. What is his clear message to you?

6. Why do you think Jesus allowed as much ambiguity as he did regarding money and possessions? Why didn't he just spell out exactly what we can or cannot own and how much wealth we can or cannot have?

7. In his book *Celebration of Discipline*, author and teacher Richard Foster unfolds some principles that can help us make strategic, Christ-honoring lifestyle choices and financial decisions. A few of those principles are summarized below. Review them and then rate yourself. On a scale of 1–10 (1 being "I rarely do this" and 10 being "I always do this") how actively are you living out these principles?

_____ Reject anything that is producing an addiction in you.

_____ Buy things for their usefulness rather than their status.

_____ Refuse to become a slave of modern gadgetry. Resist the notion that because the newest model has a new feature, you must have it.

_____ Develop a habit of giving things away. De-accumulate.

_____ Reject all "buy now, pay later" plans.

_____ Learn to enjoy things without owning them. Share things. Enjoy public parks and libraries.

_____ Develop a deeper appreciation for creation. Stimulate your senses with nature rather than just modern technology.

_____ Shun whatever would distract you from your main goal of seeking first God's kingdom.

Is there a lifestyle choice (a specific purchase or financial decision) on the front burner of your life right now? How might the above principles shape that decision? Be concrete.

8. In Matthew 13:44–46, Jesus tells two parables—one of a hidden treasure and one of a costly pearl. Carefully review both parables. What are the common threads?

NOTE: These parables are often misunderstood as examples of self-surrender and sacrifice. But that misses the point. This is not a harsh call to heroic action; it's a simple statement about relative value. The kingdom of God is the "buy" of a lifetime. Stumbling on it, any sane investor would gladly, "joyfully" cash out of lesser holdings to buy it. In the words of Randy Alcorn, "This is like a child given the chance to trade bubble gum for a new bicycle, or a man offered ownership of the Coca-Cola company in exchange for a sack of bottle caps." Author John White says this of the lucky merchant: "There is nothing noble about his sacrifice. There would on the other hand be something incredibly stupid about not making it. . . . Everyone will envy him for his good fortune and commend him not on his spiritual character but on his common sense."

9. Consider once again the words from the reading—that as members of the kingdom we are to live as ones "informed by a different view of reality." According to the two parables referred to above, what is that reality?

Do you think pursuing the kingdom really is worth it?

How would your lifestyle be different if you really believed that?

TAKE-AWAY

My summary of the main point of this session, and how it impacts me personally:

NOTE: You will fill in this information after your group discussion. Leave it blank until the conclusion of your meeting.

The Bible study portion of the next session was designed to be completed during a time of extended solitude (a few hours, minimally). We suggest you look ahead to that study and do some advanced planning to allow enough time for yourself.

SESSION
SIX

CULTIVATING A HEART
OF COMPASSION

Cultivating a Heart of Compassion

Reading adapted from a message by Lee Strobel

I t happened in Atlanta, Georgia, just a few years ago. Mary Ann Cardell, an elderly woman, was evicted from a hotel for transients when she couldn't pay the rent. She wandered late into the night trying to find someone to take her in, but the alcohol on her breath scared them off. They found her body the next morning in an empty lot along with a note she had written: "I have nowhere to go, and there is no one to understand. God is not dead. He is only sleeping, *but sleeping very soundly.*"

Our world is filled with forgotten and marginalized people.

Some two hundred years prior, a wealthy English father took his timid fifteen-year-old daughter Elizabeth past a notorious women's prison, a hellhole where inmates desperately reached out through the bars and begged and clamored for help. The little girl was so shaken by the horrendous site that she wrote in her journal, *"If this is the world, where is God?"*

Our world is filled with forgotten and marginalized people. Inmates in prisons. Immigrants who fill jobs we wouldn't want our kids to have. The mentally disabled. The poor. In other words, people who God loves. And the truth is, while God does not sleep, all too often his people do.

But two hundred years ago, Elizabeth Fry, that British teenager, fought the temptation to nap.

A Walk into Darkness

Elizabeth's story starts with that experience as a teenager that caused her to question the very existence of God. But two years later, a visiting pastor convinced her that God is real. Elizabeth was inspired by Jesus and his love for the marginalized of his day—the prostitutes, the lepers, the social outcasts, the poor. Her heart was touched by Jesus' teaching in Matthew 25 that *whatever we do for the least among us, we do for him.*

So at age seventeen, she ventured off her comfortable estate and walked among the poor in the surrounding village. Her heart went out to them. She concluded that if Christ was really alive in her life, then *she* was his hands and feet in the everyday trenches of her world.

In 1813, Elizabeth's life took a dramatic turn. It began when she heard about Newgate Prison for Women, which was even worse than the prison she had seen as a teenager. It was a hellish place. Hundreds of women and their children were crowded into a stark facility that had been built to house far fewer.

The place was filthy and foul-smelling. Disease was rampant. An average of five women died each month. There was no clothing except for the rags on their backs. No beds, only the floor. No heat, no baths. One person said going inside was like entering a pen of wild beasts.

When Elizabeth Fry asked to see the prison for herself, the authorities were aghast and tried to talk her out of it. But she persisted. As the iron door slammed behind her on the day of her first visit, the horrifying sight of the inmates broke Elizabeth's heart. She began speaking to them about the deplorable conditions. And then she asked, "Would you be pleased if someone were to come and serve you?"

The prisoners looked at each other in cynical disbelief. "And just where would we find such a friend?"

"I am your friend."

She began talking about God and how he wanted to be their friend as well. She told them they could rise above

> *She concluded that if Christ was really alive in her life, then she was his hands and feet in the everyday trenches of her world.*

their despair. They hung on every word. When finally she was about to leave, one woman cried out, "Oh, you'll never come again!"

"I *will* come again," Elizabeth replied.

And she did. Time after time. Because that first visit had done two things inside of her. First, it overwhelmed her with the huge amount of work that needed to be done. But, second, it inspired her. Because even in those brief moments, she could already see how the most hardened felon was susceptible to the love of Jesus.

Elizabeth organized other Christians to come and help nearly around the clock. They provided practical assistance and supplies, taught the Bible, trained the women, built friendships. Most of all, they treated them as people who matter to God. Inmate after inmate—seeing Jesus Christ serve them in flesh and blood—committed their lives to him.

Inmate after inmate— seeing Jesus Christ serve them in flesh and blood—committed their lives to him.

Over time, the impossible happened. Newgate was transformed. Prisoners went from spitting profanities to singing worship songs. They went from violence to turning the other cheek. They went from an "every person for herself" attitude to becoming a community. So incredible was the transformation that one prisoner later wrote, " ... I bless the day that brought me inside Newgate's walls; for it was there that the rays of Divine Truth shone into my dark heart."

Ultimately, Elizabeth founded the Protestant Sisters of Charity to help spread hope to the outcasts of society. All of Britain, and soon much of Europe, took notice. For the first time, governments began passing laws to treat prisoners humanely.

A Road Map to Compassionate Servanthood

There's something inside of me that wants to live the kind of Christlike, difference-making life that Elizabeth Fry lived. What can we learn from her? What are the qualities that can move us down the road of compassion?

First, learn from Elizabeth's *heart*. Elizabeth served others out of a heart that had first been revolutionized by Jesus. Even her sister noticed how Elizabeth began to behave differently toward others after receiving Christ.

"There was a most marked change in her. The Bible became her study, visiting the poor, her great object. To us, she was now always amiable and patient, forbearing and humble. . . . She was really and truly awakening to a new life in Jesus Christ."

The Bible says that a person cannot be the same after authentically giving his or her life to Christ. Galatians 5:22 says his Spirit, over time, transforms us to be more loving, show more kindness, demonstrate goodness and generosity. His concerns become our concerns.

Question: If you are a follower of Jesus, would your brother or sister say they've noticed a change in you? Is God transforming you so that, more and more, your heart is *his* heart? Is the stewardship of your life and resources increasingly in line with his priorities—particularly to the poor and forgotten? If not, have you *really* given yourself to him?

If you are a follower of Jesus, would your brother or sister say they've noticed a change in you?

Second, consider the *eyes* of Elizabeth Fry. She had an uncanny ability to see needs that others ignored. So here is another question: Among the people you routinely bump into, might there be subterranean needs? Might some people be quietly desperate, or on the brink financially or emotionally? What would happen if *you* learned to see your everyday world with fresh eyes—with the eyes of Jesus that peer into the nooks and crannies—and discern where there are needs you might be able to meet. Of course, you may not be able to meet all of them yourself. But are there some you could?

Finally, consider what you can learn from the *feet* of Elizabeth Fry. She didn't just remain in her own comfortable sphere. Instead, she intentionally walked into new places—among the poor and marginalized whom she would not ordinarily encounter—just as Jesus did. He too purposefully walked into places where the religious folks of his day would never venture.

Take William Booth. One night he couldn't sleep and so he decided to go for a walk through the poor section of town where he had never before ventured. He walked all night. When he returned home his wife was frantic. "Where have you been?"

"Katherine," he said, "I've been to hell. I've been to hell."

That experience prompted them in 1865 to found the Salvation Army to do something about it.

When was the last time you've been to "hell"? When was the last time you've stopped taking the safe routes and living only in the comfort of your own surroundings? Do you ever venture out to see and experience the hidden suffering of the forgotten people? Are you willing to move out of isolation and toward some people in need—close enough to learn their names, know their stories, even become friends? Often it takes the movement of our feet and a willingness to let our eyes see need in order to begin cultivating a heart of compassion.

It's the great upside-down truth. Jesus came not to be served but to serve.

Awakening to God's Call

Although God doesn't sleep, there are times when I do. But I'll tell you what: Elizabeth Fry has been a wake-up call for me.

Do you sense him rousing you? Is he trying to do an awakening work in your heart? It may not involve anything as elaborate as Elizabeth's work. It may start with a cup of cold water given in his name—a small act of kindness done with great love.

Here's the ironic thing. When Elizabeth died in 1845, she had a heart that was full to the brim. The more she brought Jesus to others, the closer she got to Jesus herself. The more she poured her soul out, the more God refilled it to overflowing.

It's the great upside-down truth. Jesus came not to be served but to serve. And when we follow him, we find that unique fulfillment that only he can provide.

SPIRITUAL EXERCISE

You might call it the "proximity factor." It plays itself out with remarkable consistency. Hang out in a shopping mall and you'll probably end up spending money. Spend time in a bowling alley, and sooner or later you'll want to bowl. Sit in a bakery and you'll likely end up eating sweets.

The proximity factor is equally true when it comes to compassion. Allow yourself to see need, and eventually you'll want to help. Maintain your distance, and you probably won't.

Your assignment this week is to *get near the needy*. Do *something* to move out of the comfort of isolation. You will have to figure out how this can work for you. Here are just a few ideas.

- Begin by noticing. As you read the paper or watch the news this week, pay attention to the needy and marginalized. Imagine if their circumstances became yours. Pray for them.
- As you're driving to and from work, consider going through neighborhoods of a lower economic standing. Real people with real feelings live in those places. Ask God to open your heart to these people.
- Sign up for a day of serving in an area of need. Visit a nursing home. Help out a food pantry with a load of groceries.
- Stop to talk to a few street people. Ask their names. Ask them about their stories. Consider buying them a meal.
- Pay attention to forgotten people who you tend to "look beyond" every day. Look them in the eye and bless them with a sincere and respectful word of encouragement or act of kindness.
- Open your wallet. Specifically ask God to use your money and possessions. Make an anonymous gift to a family that is struggling financially or sign up to provide monthly support for a third-world child.

Don't worry about trying to make a big impact. Just do *something* to move closer to the needy and extend a loving hand. Then notice what happens to you in the process.

BIBLE STUDY

T his week's Bible study is designed to be experienced as part of a time of solitude—we suggest a few hours minimally, at a time when you will be fairly rested and alert. (If it is not possible to set aside that amount of time, plan to reflect on the passage below during several sittings throughout the week.)

Find a place where you will be alone, comfortable, and free from distractions and interruptions. It might be helpful to pick a location where you can get up and go for a walk along the way. Be sure to bring your Bible and a journal or notepad for writing down your thoughts. The outline below is to help guide you, but by all means follow the Holy Spirit as he prompts you. The goal is not to complete an assignment; the goal is to quiet yourself before God and hear him speak to you about a subject that is very dear to his heart.

Still Yourself

One of the hardest things to do in our daily busyness is simply to *stop*. Being quiet usually produces boredom, anxiety, or drowsiness. But in order to embark on this exercise, you must deliberately be still. Don't trouble yourself with what you have to do later or what happened yesterday. If these thoughts pop up along the way, "park" them on your pad of paper so they don't interfere with your concentration.

Invite God's Presence

Acknowledge that God is present with you right now. Thank him for his never-failing companionship. Place yourself in his hands. Ask him to help you be sensitive to his leadings.

Open Yourself to Being Washed by the Word

Scripture says that we are to be washed by the Word (Eph. 5:25–27). Think of what happens when something gets washed. Soap and water move through the fibers of the dirty fabric at the deepest level, lifting out impurities and removing them from the fabric. Only after washing can we see the fabric in the state in which it was originally designed.

Invite God to wash your mind and thoughts even if it stings a little bit. Resolve that you will not read merely to increase your knowledge, or to have something profound to report to your group. Read with a readiness to surrender. Resolve to be obedient to his Word.

Meditate on the Passage

The focal point of this reflection time is Matthew 25:31–46. These are the words Jesus spoke during a private time with his disciples, just days before his death.

1. Read the passage several times in its entirety. Read it slowly, writing down any words or phrases that stand out to you.

2. What emotions are being stirred in you?

3. Try to imagine the scene that Jesus is describing. Imagine yourself serving a marginalized person—someone considered "the least" by our society—a homeless person, perhaps. Imagine feeding them, clothing them, welcoming them, tending to their illness, lavishing care on them. What thoughts or feelings does that picture evoke? Does it make you comfortable or uncomfortable?

4. Now imagine learning that—although you didn't know it at the time—it was Jesus that you were actually feeding, clothing, welcoming, caring for. What thoughts or feelings does that evoke?

5. Read the passage once more. Be quiet before God. Listen. What do you sense he is saying to you through the passage?

6. As you bring this time to a close, respond to this question: How would your life be different if you *really believed* you were serving Christ as you served the poor and needy?

How would it change the way you spend your time?

How would it change the way you spend your money?

TAKE-AWAY

My summary of the main point of this session, and how it impacts me personally:

NOTE: You will fill in this information after your group discussion. Leave it blank until the conclusion of your meeting.

SESSION
SEVEN

The Chance of a Lifetime

Reading adapted from a message by John Ortberg

There is an odd tendency in human beings to think we can worm our way out of the consequences of our actions. If you've ever tried to finesse a police officer out of a traffic ticket, you know. This tendency starts very early in life.

We were at dinner one night and one of our children was being very squirrelly—clearly headed for trouble. We issued a warning: "Settle down or there will be serious consequences." Then there was a spill—of Exxon Valdez proportions. Just as we were about to administer the consequences, this child, with a gleam in the eyes, pulled a dollar out of a pocket and said, "Maybe Mr. Washington can change your mind!"

There is One before whom we will all stand, every one of us. This One is loving and holy and gracious and just, and he intends for us to understand that we really will give an account of our lives. We will not be able to finesse our way around his throne. Mr. Washington will not change his mind.

To reinforce this truth, Jesus tells a story of three servants in Matthew 25:14–30. Three threads run through this story, each with something important to teach us about the Master.

The Lord of the Gift

The first theme is wonderful news: God, the Master, is an amazingly generous person. In those days there were no corporations as we know them today. Wealth was

There is an odd tendency in human beings to think we can worm our way out of the consequences of our actions.

concentrated in just a few rich households, and this was one of them.

The master in the parable gathers three of his employees around him. Then an extraordinary thing happens. He entrusts vast sums of money to them. One talent—the basic currency of the day—was worth essentially fifteen years of a worker's wages. Now, in those days, people basically lived from day to day. To have accumulated just one year's worth of wages was an enormous amount of wealth. So the figures Jesus is using are staggering.

Then, after entrusting his wealth to these servants, the master goes away. And it dawns on the servants. This is a chance of a lifetime.

Most people can tell of a moment when they had the chance of a lifetime. For me it came during graduate school. I was a part-time pastor at a church. I was going to be getting married soon. I desperately needed money to pay off my school debts and to go on the kind of honeymoon I had always dreamed of.

After entrusting his wealth to these servants, the master goes away. And it dawns on the servants. This is a chance of a lifetime.

The only way I could think of to come up with that kind of money was to go on a game show. So I did. I went on a show called "Tic-Tac-Dough." It had a great big tic-tac-toe board, and each square on that board had a question from some category. If you got it right, you would get your X or O.

I ended up in a game with another guy. The questions were so easy that neither of us missed any. Every time there was a tie game, the jackpot went up by thousands of dollars. We had five tie games. Finally, he missed a question, and I had two Xs in a row. All I needed was one right answer and I would have more money than I had ever seen in my life—the honeymoon of my dreams.

I waited to see what category would come up in this square that I needed to win, hoping it would be something that I knew—like maybe the Bible. The category came up: *mixed drinks!* Then the question came up. "What is the drink that's made up of two shots of scotch and a half shot of sweet vermouth?"

Suddenly it occurred to me, "I'm a Baptist pastor. I'm in trouble if I get this wrong and I'm in trouble if I get it right."

We honeymooned in Wisconsin. It was a chance of a lifetime, and I blew it.

In Jesus' story, the lord of the gift gave a chance of a lifetime. The first servant recognizes that. We are told he "went off at once." He realized that he would be insane to let anything keep him away from this chance of a lifetime.

It is important to note that there are no "no-talent" people in the parable. There are people with varying numbers of talents, but there are no "no-talent" people.

And there are no "no-talent" people reading this page. The truth is, the Master has been very generous with *you*. He has entrusted his property to you. He has given you money, possessions, time, abilities. And his offer is still open. You may invest in his kingdom. Others have come before you who "went off at once" and others will come after you. But this is *your* day.

The Lord of the gift has given you the chance of a lifetime. And he wonders, what are you going to do?

The Lord of the gift has given you the chance of a lifetime. And he wonders, what are you going to do?

The Lord of the Settled Account

This brings us to the second major thread in this story—the thread of accountability. It is quite clear that the lord of the gift, although he has gone away for a long time, is coming back. Jesus says, "After a long time, the master of the slaves came and settled accounts with them."

The master in the story takes the settling of accounts with dead seriousness. He goes through it with the first servant and then the second servant. The results are different, but because each gave it their best, the reward is the same. But then he gets to the third servant. At this point things get dark.

The one who had received the one talent came forward. Having hidden his talent in the ground, he returned it. "Here is what belongs to you."

The master responds, "You wicked and lazy servant."

Wicked and lazy. Those are two words we don't use much today. But Jesus assures us that humans are capable of being them, so we better take them seriously. They are the sin of unrealized potential—the willful refusal to invest the good gifts of God for the glory of the Giver; the willful refusal to choose risk and obedience and to choose comfort and safety instead.

Jesus is clear. What you do with your life and resources matters to him. It matters to the world that desperately needs what the Lord of the gift offers. His strong language does not run counter to the notion of grace. In fact, his words are a result of love. Jesus doesn't want you to get to the end of your life and know the profound regret of missing the chance of a lifetime.

The Lord of the Reward

Jesus is clear. What you do with your life and resources matters to him.

Finally, we come to the last thread of the story. The lord of the gift, the lord of the settled account, is also the lord of the lavish reward.

When the master in this tale comes back and finds faithful servants in the time of final reckoning, he says those wonderful words, "Well done, good and faithful servant."

Words of affirmation are a powerful force. The prospect of being praised, particularly by someone important to us, brings disproportionate joy. The lack of praise brings disproportionate disappointment. For better, and sometimes worse, we hunger for affirmation.

Think about standing before the God of creation. Imagine God looking at your life and then looking you in the eye and saying, "Well done. You were faithful. You diligently invested what I entrusted to you. I'm proud of you. Enter my joy!" What words could you ever want to hear more than those?

Words of praise. The offer of everlasting joy. But there's something else. It's striking what the master does not say at this point. He does not say, "Well done, good and faithful servant. Now you can float on lovely clouds and sing in the choir for a hundred billion years."

He says, "You have been faithful with a few things. I will put you in charge of many things" (Matt. 25:23). In the parallel passage in Luke 19, he says to one servant, "You take charge of ten cities" (v. 17). To another, "You take charge of five cities" (v. 19).

There's irony in this part of the story. "You have been trustworthy in a *few* things." What? Greater wealth than they had ever seen? More money than they could have imagined? Just a few things? Yes. Compared to what's coming next.

Think about this. Compared to what's coming next, the wealth of Bill Gates, the power of Napoleon, the fame of Michael Jordan, constitute "a few things." Whatever you invest for the Master this side of heaven will look like just a few things—pocket change—when compared to the "hundredfold" reward promised in heaven (Matt.19:29).

The master always entrusts the trustworthy with more.

But there is still more. After welcoming, praising, enfolding in everlasting joy, and entrusting with exponentially magnified wealth, the Master will place every faithful servant in charge of "many things." The Master always entrusts the trustworthy with more.

In the book of Revelation, Christ says it this way: "To the one who overcomes . . ." (that is, to every trustworthy servant) ". . . I will give a place with me on my throne" (Rev. 3:21 NRSV).

Imagine yourself sitting with Christ on his throne. Imagine, if you can, reigning with him. Partnering with him in his eternal work. Imagine fulfilling your ultimate assignment—the purpose for which you were created—at the side of Christ.

If you are faithful now, when the Lord of the gift returns, you surely will.

SPIRITUAL EXERCISE

One of the biggest hindrances to faithful stewardship is our chronic failure to see our present lives through the lenses of eternity.

Martin Luther, the sixteenth-century reformer, said he had only two days on his calendar: *today* and *That Day (the day of reckoning)*. Your spiritual exercise is to live this week with those two days before you. Write "today" and "That Day" on cards and place them in strategic places—your calendar, your wallet, you car visor, your desk, etc.

As you go about your daily routines, as you make moment-to-moment choices concerning your money and possessions, as you engage in relationships, as you expend time and energy, continually come back to the question: Am I investing *today* in light of *That Day?*

Observe what difference it makes to live your life this way. Make a few notes here to discuss with your group.

Let me assume the role of "eternal financial counselor" and offer this advice: choose your investments carefully; compare their rates of interest; consider their ultimate trustworthiness; and especially compare how they will be working for you a few million years from now.

—Randy Alcorn, *Money, Possessions and Eternity*

T ake a closer look at the Parable of the Talents (Matt. 25:14–30). Read the passage several times on your own before moving on to the questions.

1. The story begins with the claim that the servants are managers of someone else's money. Randy Alcorn writes: "God is not just the owner of the universe in general, but the owner of me in particular. In fact, I am twice his—first by creation, and second by redemption."

   What is your reaction to the thought that your wealth—even your body and soul—are really God's property?

   Does this increase or decrease your desire to use your life and resources for his cause? Why?

2. The master gives each servant varying amounts of money. Although the text isn't specific, what might the foolish servant have said about the master and his treatment of the other two servants?

Describe a time, if any, when someone else's greater resources (financial or otherwise) discouraged you and perhaps felt unfair. What helped you get beyond it? (Are you beyond it?)

How might those thoughts—if left unchecked—lead you down a path similar to the one described in verse 18?

> NOTE: At the end of your life, God will not ask you why you didn't lead somebody else's life. God will not ask you why you did not use someone else's resources. He will not ask, "What did you do with what you did not have?" He will ask you, "What did you do with what you had?"

3. It's easy to think, "What I have is too small to matter." Or, "If I just had more I'd invest more in God's kingdom." But through the repeated words of the master, Jesus brings to light a key principal in this regard. What is it? (see vv. 21, 23)

What insight does Luke 21:1–4 shed on the subject?

In Luke 16:10–13, Jesus elaborates further. Summarize his point in your own words.

4. The third servant is judged quite harshly. How do you react to this judgment (Matt. 25:26–30)?

The servant is not judged for doing desperately bad things. He did not steal, embezzle, or defraud. He is judged for doing *nothing*. Why do you think God gets so angry at the waste of human potential?

Does this part of the story stir any concern in you? When it comes to your own stewardship, is there any wasted potential in your own life that could cause a similar response in the Master? Describe.

5. What tactic does the servant use to transfer the blame (vv. 24–25)?

NOTE: The servant's response is a smoke screen—an attempt to evade accountability. "Don't blame me, it's your fault. I was afraid of you so I hid the money." It is interesting that the master doesn't directly contradict the servant. Instead, he makes the point that if the servant was simply afraid of his accountability to the master, at least he would have gotten interest on the money. The master knew that fear wasn't the core issue. Wicked and lazy was the proper diagnosis.

How inclined are you to transfer blame with respect to your own stewardship? How does that usually manifest itself?

6. Our motivation for good stewardship should always be rooted in gratitude, coupled with the earnest desire to be found faithful. Yet the Bible also appeals to the incentive of rewards. Summarize what you learn about God and his rewards in the following passages:

Matthew 19:28–29

1 Corinthians 3:8–14

Hebrews 11:24–26

Galatians 6:7–9

NOTE: Because some of us were raised within a system that taught God's love was conditional upon our works, the idea of God giving us rewards leads to confusion. An understanding of God as a giver of grace conflicts with that old picture of him as dispensing good things to good people and bad things to bad people. To get past this confusion, we need to remind ourselves of the ultimate reason God made us: to be in relationship with him. That connection is not something we can earn or demand. We can only accept it on the merits of Christ, knowing it is God's earnest desire to be intimate with us. Every reward we ever get from him must be understood ultimately as the increased capacity to enjoy him. He doesn't give us "stuff" to reward us—that's not what we need. Any blessing—either here or in heaven—will only, in the final analysis, have as its purpose to draw us into closer communion with the One who is our soul's completion.

7. Even though the road to discipleship is paved with self-denial (Mark 8:34–36), paradoxically, it is also the best way to live here and now. (As it states in John 10:10, "I have come that they may have life, and have it to the full.") Explain in your own words how you believe this is possible.

8. In rewarding the two faithful servants, it is significant that the master did not say, "Well said" or "well believed," but "well *done*." This brings us back to the core premise of this study: It is what we actually *do* with our money and possessions that reveals what we actually *believe*. Being as candid as possible, summarize what you really believe—based on your actions— concerning:

God's ownership of all that you have

Your role as a manager and investor

The reality of future accountability

The promise of future rewards

9. As you reflect back on this entire study on good stewardship, in what way has the Spirit most affirmed your beliefs and actions? In what way have your beliefs and actions been most challenged?

What three steps can you take toward further growth in these areas?

TAKE-AWAY

My summary of the main point of this session, and how it impacts me personally:

NOTE: You will fill in this information after your group discussion. Leave it blank until the conclusion of your meeting.

Leader's Guide

How to Use This Discussion Guide

Doers of the Word

One of the reasons small groups are so effective is because when people are face-to-face, they can discuss and process information instead of merely listening passively. *God's truths are transforming only to the extent they are received and absorbed.* Just as uneaten food cannot nourish, truth "out there"—either in a book or spoken by a teacher—cannot make a difference if it is undigested. Even if it is bitten off and chewed, it must be swallowed and made part of each cell to truly give life.

The spiritual transformation at the heart of this Bible study series can occur only if people get truth and make that truth part of their lives. Reading about sit-ups leaves you flabby; doing sit-ups gives you strong abdominals. That's why in every session, we present group members with exercises to do during the week. They also study Scripture on their own in (hopefully) unhurried settings where they can meditate on and ponder the truths that are encountered. Group discussion is the other way we've designed for them to grab hold of these important lessons.

This study is not a correspondence course. It's a personal and group experience designed to help believers find a biblical approach to their spiritual lives that really works. We recognize that people have a variety of learning styles, so we've tried to incorporate a variety of ways to learn. One of the most important ways they will learn is when they meet together to process the information verbally in a group.

Not Question-by-Question

One approach to learning used by some small groups encourages members to systematically discuss *everything* they learn on their own during the group time. Such material is designed so group members do a study and then report what their answers were for each question. While this approach is thorough, it can become boring. The method we've adopted includes individual study, but we do not suggest discussing *everything* in the session when you meet. Instead, questions are given to leaders (hence, this Leader's Guide) to get at the heart of the material without being rote recitations of the answers the members came up with on their own. This may be a bit confusing at first, because some people fill in the blanks, expecting each answer to be discussed, and discussed in the order they wrote them down. Instead, you, as a leader, will be asking questions *based* on their study, but not necessarily numerically corresponding to their study. We think this technique of handling the sessions has the best of both approaches: individual learning is reinforced in the group setting without becoming wearisome.

It is also important that you understand you will not be able to cover all the material provided each week. We give you more than you can use in every session—not to frustrate you, but to give you enough so you can pick and choose. *Base your session plan on the needs of individual members of your group.*

There may be a few times when the material is so relevant to your group members that every question seems to fit. Don't feel bad about taking two weeks on a session. The purpose of this series is transformational life-change, not timely book completion!

Getting Ready for *Your* Group

We suggest that to prepare for a meeting, you first do the study yourself and spend some time doing the spiritual exercise. Then look over the questions we've given you in the Leader's Guide. As you consider your group members and the amount of discussion time you have, ask yourself if the questions listed for that session relate to your group's needs. Would some other questions fit better? We've tried to highlight the main points of each session, but you may feel you need to hit some aspect harder than we did, or not spend as much time on a point. As long as your preparation is based on knowledge of your group, customize the session however you see fit.

As we pointed out, you may have to adapt the material because of time considerations. It is very hard to discuss every topic in a given session in detail—we certainly don't recommend it. You may also only have a limited time because of the nature of your group. Again, the purpose isn't to cover every question exhaustively, but to get the main point across in each session (whatever incidental discussion may otherwise occur). As a guide to your preparation, review the *Primary Focus* statement at the beginning and the *Session Highlights* paragraph at the end of each session's Leader's Guide. They represent our attempt to summarize what we were trying to get across in writing the sessions. If your questions get at those points, you're on the right track.

A Guide, Not a Guru

Now a word about your role as leader. We believe all small groups need a leader. While it is easy to see that a group discussion would get off track without a facilitator, we would like you to ponder another very important reason you hold the position you do.

This Bible study series is about spiritual growth—about Christ being formed in each of us. One of the greatest gifts you can give another person is to pay attention to his or her spiritual life. As a leader, you will serve your group members by observing their lives and trying to hear, in the questions they ask and the answers they give, where they are in their spiritual development. Your discerning observations are an invaluable contribution to their spiritual progress. That attention, prayer, and insight is an extremely rare gift—but it is revolutionary for those blessed enough to have such a person in their lives. You are that person. You give that gift. You can bring that blessing.

People desperately need clarity about spirituality. Someone needs to blow away the fog that surrounds the concept of what it means to live a spiritual life and give believers concrete ideas how to pursue it. Spiritual life is just *life*. It's that simple. Christ-followers must invite God into all aspects of life, even the everyday routines. That is where we spend most of our time anyway, so that is where we must be with God. If not, the Christian life will become pretense, or hypocrisy. We must decompartmentalize life so that we share it all with God in a barrier-free union with him.

We say all this so that you, the leader, can be encouraged in and focused on your role. You are the person observing how people are doing. You are the one who detects the doors people will not let God through, the one who sees the blind spots they don't, the one who gently points out the unending patience of God who will not stop working in us until "his work is completed" (Phil. 1:6). You will hold many secret conversations with God about the people in your group—while you meet, during a phone call, sitting across the table at lunch, when you're alone. In addition to making the meeting happen, this is one of the most important things you can do to be a catalyst for life-change. That is why you're meeting together anyway—to see people become more like Christ. If you lead as a *facilitator* of discussion, not a teacher, and a *listener* rather than the one who should be listened to, you will see great changes in the members of your group.

Money: Why Is It So Important to God?

Primary Focus: To understand the "spiritual" nature of money and possessions.

Remember that these questions do not correspond numerically with the questions in the assignment. We do not recommend simply going over what your group members put for their answers—that will probably result in a tedious discussion at best. Rather, use some or all of these questions (and perhaps some of your own) to stimulate discussion; that way, you'll be processing the content of the session from a fresh perspective each meeting.

1. *(Regarding question 1 in the Bible study)* What was the "story" of your family with respect to money and possessions? What early experiences growing up still affect your views and practices today?

2. If you are married, what are some areas of agreement you and your spouse have about money management? What are some areas of struggle for the two of you?

   If you are not married, what do you believe are some specific areas of strength in your personal money management? What are some weaknesses?

NOTE: Money is one of the most volatile issues among married people. This question may uncover some areas of deep pain. As a leader, be tuned in to that possibility. Don't try to handle deep-seated financial problems alone. Encourage anyone in your group who has problems in this area to get help from a financial or Christian counselor (or both).

---

3. As the reading mentioned, when Zacchaeus encountered the love of Christ, it radically altered his perspective on his possessions. To what degree has your use of money been altered by Christ's presence in your life? Be specific.

4. As you engaged in the spiritual exercise this week, what observations did you make about your thoughts and feelings concerning money and possessions?

5. *(Regarding question 3 in the Bible study)* How do you resolve the tension of the two themes in Proverbs and Matthew?

6. *(Regarding question 4 in the Bible study)* How have you seen the love of money affect your life?

7. The reading mentioned that the Bible contains an arsenal of verses about money, many of which we avoid or skim over. What passages (or topics) in the Bible relating to good stewardship are you dreading talking about in this study? Why?

NOTE: People may have some trouble being completely open about their fears. Don't push too hard to get them to be vulnerable. If you have a group that is more inclined to be open, by all means have people share from the heart. But if that's not the case, don't be discouraged. This is a very sensitive topic— as the study progresses, more opportunities will arise for in-depth discussion.

---

8. *(Regarding question 9 in the Bible study)* What connection do you see between money, possessions, and *your* spiritual life?

9. *(Regarding question 10 in the Bible study)* What do you want to see happen in your life through the course of this study? Is there anything you would like to do differently?

Take-Away: At the conclusion of your discussion each week, take a few minutes to have group members sum up the session and its impact on them by filling in the Take-Away section at the end of each session. Don't tell them what they are supposed to write—let them be true to their own experiences. When they have written their summaries, have everyone share with the others what they wrote. Statements should be similar to the statements in Session Highlights. If you feel the whole group may have missed an important aspect of the session, be sure to bring that up in the closing discussion.

Session Highlights: Money management is a predominant theme in Scripture; money is a litmus test of character; what we avoid facing in the area of money and possessions tells us a lot about ourselves; spiritual transformation is impossible without changing our attitudes and use of money and possessions.

NOTE: In Session 6, the spiritual exercise encourages individuals to take a risk and get close to human need. A great way to augment this assignment is to schedule a serving opportunity as a group. You may want to do some advance planning now. Identify a project you could all do together and estimate when you will be covering that session. Reserve that date with group members so, if possible, your serving project coincides with that session. (Of course, even if it doesn't coincide, it will be a valuable experience.)

SESSION TWO

The Open Hands of God

Primary Focus: To ground our good stewardship in the generous nature of God.

1. *(Regarding question 1 in the Bible study)* Briefly relate to the group your experience receiving lavish generosity from someone. What did you conclude about the lasting impact of such acts?

2. Share some observations you made during your spiritual exercise about noticing God's generosity.

3. *(Regarding question 2 in the Bible study)* What stood out most in your study of Psalm 65? What would you add to that psalm if you were writing it?

4. There can be times when we are disappointed in God and believe he hasn't done enough for us. In what ways are you sometimes tempted to believe God has been stingy or inadequate toward you?

5. *(Regarding question 4 in the Bible study)* What do you think would happen if you tried to become more mature in your walk with God by being a good steward, but lost sight of his generosity?

6. *(Regarding question 5 in the Bible study)* How is your life different today because Jesus chose to release instead of grasp?

7. *(Regarding question 6 in the Bible study)* What factors contribute to your tendency to assert your rights or protect your turf with respect to money or possessions? In what ways have you become more or less generous in the last year?

8. *(Regarding question 7 in the Bible study)* How do you react to the statement that our handling of money and possessions reveals what we *really* believe? What connection do you see between your generosity and your belief about God's generosity?

Session Highlights: By nature we are clutchers, but that is not true of God; God designed us to enjoy material blessings as well as spiritual ones; when we dwell on God's generosity, it is easier to be generous ourselves.

NOTE: The spiritual exercise in the next session (Session 3) will require each member to sit down with his or her financial records from the past month or two for the purpose of observation and reflection. You may want to look ahead to that exercise and alert your group to it.

SESSION THREE

Tithing: A Training Exercise for the Heart

Primary Focus: To understand the importance tithing has in cultivating a life of faith.

1. Describe a time in the past when you found yourself a slave of the wrong master (money). How did you get free? If you've never felt that enslavement, what has kept you liberated?

2. What did you discover as you looked back over your financial records for the last month or two?

NOTE: Again, be careful not to press for a level of disclosure that individuals or the group may not be ready for. (For example, insisting that everyone present their checkbooks for review would not be wise unless you have a very close group with lots of history and established trust.) Self-disclosure must unfold naturally. One-on-one settings may be the best option for sensitive follow-up conversations.

---

3. The reading mentioned how the "more monster" bombards us every day. Which of the *more* messages in our culture is especially seductive for you right now?

4. *(Regarding question 4 in the Bible study)* What practice in our own day might be similar to the offering of blemished lambs in Malachi's time? What beliefs about God underlie someone's attempt to make such offerings? What beliefs about one's self might lead to such a practice?

5. *(Regarding question 4 in the Bible study)* What do you think of God's offer to put him to the test in the matter of tithing? What do you think God wants you to do personally with his challenge? What fear or anxiety surrounds taking this step?

6. *(Regarding question 6 in the Bible study)* What is your reaction to the statement that the tithe is a floor, not a ceiling?

7. *(Regarding question 7 in the Bible study)* How do you think giving reveals your heart? How do you think it can shape your heart?

Session Highlights: Tithing is an effective tool to dethrone money as our God; tithing is God's idea—it reveals and shapes our heart; tithing is a floor, not a ceiling; God invites us to tithe as a way to test his faithfulness.

NOTE: Remember that Session 6 relates to getting near to those in need. If you want to do something together as a group to fulfill this assignment, you'll need to plan something soon. It will probably be too late to coordinate everybody's schedule if you wait until you get to that session.

SESSION FOUR

Behind the Scenes of Debt

Primary Focus: To discover the character issues that can lead to unhealthy debt and to overcome them.

1. What was the verse you memorized in your spiritual exercise this week? How did it go trying to call it to mind as you made various purchases? Did you postpone any purchases? If so, what happened after the twenty-four-hour cooling-off period?

2. *(Regarding question 1 in the Bible study)* What are some of the words or phrases you used to describe the slavery of debt? Which of those have you personally experienced at some point?

3. *(Regarding question 2 in the Bible study)* Which of the verses in Proverbs impacted you the most? Why?

4. *(Regarding question 3 in the Bible study)* What is your level of contentment these days in the area of money and possessions? What is at the root of your condition, either good or bad?

5. *(Regarding question 4 in the Bible study)* How did Paul's teaching in 1 Timothy 6 help you in your struggle to be clear about needs and wants?

6. *(Regarding question 5 in the Bible study)* What connections might be made between a person's view of God and his or her ability to stay out of debt? How has your view of God affected your indebtedness (or lack of it)?

7. *(Regarding question 6 in the Bible study)* Do you ever pray for what you covet? Why or why not? What do you need to do to avoid exposing yourself to what you covet?

8. *(Regarding question 7 in the Bible study)* What character issues did you decide to address related to debt? What is your plan to get out of debt (if you are currently in debt) and get on the positive side of interest (saving)?

Session Highlights: Debt is foolish; often it has its roots in issues of character—lack of contentment, impatience, an unwillingness to trust God, envy; removal of debt leads to great freedom and helps you move to the positive side of the interest equation (saving).

A Word about Leadership: Remember the comments at the beginning of this discussion guide about your role as a leader? About now, it's probably a good idea to remind yourself that one of your key functions is to be a cheerleader—someone who seeks out signs of spiritual progress in others and makes some noise about it.

What have you seen God doing in your group members' lives as a result of this study? Don't assume they've seen that progress—and definitely don't assume they are beyond needing simple words of encouragement. Find ways to point out to people the growth you've seen. Let them know it's happening, and that it's noticable to you and others.

There aren't a whole lot of places in the world where people's spiritual progress is going to be recognized and celebrated. After all, wouldn't you like to hear someone cheer *you* on? So would your group members. You have the power to make a profound impact through a sincere, insightful remark.

Be aware, also, that some groups get sidetracked by a difficult member or situation that hasn't been confronted. And some individuals *could* be making significant progress—they just need a nudge. Encouragement is not about just saying nice things; it's about offering *words that urge*. It's about giving courage (en-*courage*-ment) to those who lack it.

So, take a risk. Say what needs to be said to encourage your members toward their goals of becoming fully devoted followers.

What Is a Biblical Lifestyle?

Primary Focus: To realize that God does not give us a mechanical lifestyle checklist but calls us to seek first his kingdom with all our resources.

1. *(Regarding question 1 in the Bible study)* What is the specific tension area you identified, and how have you managed it?

2. How did the spiritual exercise affect you this week? Describe any notable moments when you felt the Spirit's tug in the midst of a choice you had to make.

3. *(Regarding questions 2 and 3 in the Bible study)* Based on your study and reflections, what do you conclude is Jesus' command to all believers? Do you sense any specific changes toward which he is nudging you?

4. *(Regarding questions 4 and 5 in the Bible study)* How does the comparison game work in your life when it comes to lifestyle issues? How prone are you to judgmental attitudes regarding other people's lifestyles?

5. *(Regarding question 6 in the Bible study)* How does the following quote from Randy Alcorn's book *Money, Possessions and Eternity* compare with your answer to question 6?

When it comes to our attitude toward wealth, Jesus gave commands. When it comes to our specific possessions and life-style he gave us principles. Jesus did not hand us a precise checklist of what we can and cannot own, and how we can or cannot spend money. Jesus did not say just one thing about money and possessions. He said many things. They were not random clashing noises, but carefully composed melody and harmony to which we must carefully listen as we develop our life-styles. If he gave us a checklist we would not have to depend prayerfully and thoughtfully on him to guide us into the kind of life-style that pleases him.

6. *(Regarding question 7 in the Bible study)* What was your reaction to Foster's list? Which principle are you going to apply to a specific decision you are currently facing?

7. *(Regarding question 9 in the Bible study)* What lingering doubts keep you from believing that ordering your life around kingdom pursuits really is a better, richer way to live? What changes would people see in you if you lived truly and convincingly "informed by a different view of reality"?

8. How would you "seek first the kingdom" with all of your resources?

Session Highlights: We can err believing that money is automatically good, or that it is automatically bad; wealth may be a blessing, but it can easily lead to materialism; a "wartime mentality"—seeking first the kingdom—can help us steer through the minefield of choosing a God-honoring lifestyle; we must adopt a different view of reality or we will only make external changes.

NOTE: Be sure to alert your group members that the Bible study for the upcoming session requires them to have an extended time of solitude (a few hours minimally). If you think your group members may not do this on their own, you might consider scheduling an extended meeting when the group members actually do the solitude study together (alone, of course, but at the same location). You would then have the discussion immediately following or the next time the group meets.

SESSION SIX

Cultivating a Heart of Compassion

Primary Focus: To see the compassionate use of resources as normal for every believer.

1. Elizabeth Fry was transformed by Christ into a more compassionate person in a way that was observable to those around her. How might people around you say Christ has changed your attitude toward those in need? Be specific. Where do you still need to change?

2. How did it go this week as you tried to notice people in need? What kinds of things did you observe?

3. What did you feel when you stepped out to help someone? What did you learn about yourself as you took that action?

4. What are some of your fears regarding getting more involved in a compassionate lifestyle? What's at risk for you?

5. Share some of the fruit of your study and observations from the passage this week. Is there an issue that came up about which you would like to get further clarification?

6. What causes you to avoid involvement with those in need in spite of the overwhelming scope of human suffering?

NOTE: When thinking about responding to human suffering, it is easy to go on mental and emotional overload because of the sheer magnitude of the problems in our world. That overwhelmed feeling can actually lead us away from taking action—to a "What's the use?" mind-set.

There is a familiar story about a young boy who went to the beach after a huge tropical storm. Thousands of starfish had washed ashore. One by one he picked them up and started carrying them back to the ocean to keep them alive.

A cynical man walked by and said, "There are thousands of starfish dying on the beach. Do you really think you're making a difference?"

Holding a starfish in his hand, the boy replied, "Well, I'm pretty sure I'm making a difference to this one!"

Our assistance to even one person—whether through our time, our talents, or our material resources—may not change the world, but may change the world for that person.

Session Highlights: We cannot follow a compassionate Savior without imitating his compassion; we must get near suffering and poverty to change it and to change our own heart; how we treat others, especially the marginalized, is how we treat Jesus.

SESSION SEVEN

The Chance of a Lifetime

Primary Focus: To manage ourselves and our money in the light of eternity.

1. What happened as you experimented with keeping "today" and "That Day" in focus this week? Were there any surprises?

2. *(Regarding question 1 of the Bible study)* Is it threatening in any way for you to think of yourself and all you own as belonging to God? Why or why not?

NOTE: After your discussion of this question, you might want to read the following passage from Richard Foster's book, *The Challenge of the Disciplined Life.*

God's ownership of all things actually enhances our relationship with him. When we know—truly know—that the earth is the Lord's, then property itself makes us more aware of God. For example, if we were staying in and caring for the vacation home of a famous actress, we would be reminded of her daily by the very fact of living in her home. A thousand things would bring her presence to mind. So it is in our relationship with God. The house we live in is his house, the car we drive is his car, the garden we plant is his garden. We are only temporary stewards of things that belong to Another.

---

3. *(Regarding question 2 in the Bible study)* What do you think about God's fairness toward you when it comes to financial resources?

4. *(Regarding question 3 in the Bible study)* What is the key principle that Jesus brings to light? Which is harder for you: to be faithful with little or faithful with much?

5. *(Regarding question 4 in the Bible study)* How did you react to the judgment the third servant received? Why, in your opinion, is wasted potential such a disappointment for God?

6. *(Regarding question 5 in the Bible study)* In what ways are you sometimes inclined to transfer blame with respect to your stewardship?

7. *(Regarding question 7 in the Bible study)* In your view, how is it possible to follow Jesus on the road of self-denial and delayed gratification, yet at the same time experience "life to the full"?

8. *(Regarding questions 8 and 9 in the Bible study)* Summarize how this study has helped you to see what you really believe about being a good steward. What are some steps you'll be taking to become a better steward? How can this group help?

NOTE: You may want to end your final session with the following exercise. When you've finished discussing the last question, explain that you'd like everyone to pull out their house or apartment keys. Have everyone place their keys together on a table. Next have them pull out their car keys and likewise have them put those in the middle together. Now have them pull out their wallets, checkbooks, credit cards, or any other symbols of their material wealth that they happen to have with them. Pile these together with the keys.

Tell the group that this represents their collective wealth. Houses, cars, bank accounts, earning potential—it is probably a huge amount of money if it were added all together. Now, as a group, pray a prayer of commitment. Have everyone bow and offer a prayer yielding all they have or ever will have to God. Surrender everything—whether it will be given away or kept—into the gracious and guiding hands of the One who gave it all. End by commending everyone to God's grace—that each person would fulfill the commitment he or she has made to being a good steward.

Session Highlights: God is a generous Master who expects us to use what he has given us; we will be accountable for how we manage our lives, including our finances; great reward awaits us if we serve him well; we must learn to live "today" in light of "That Day."

John C. Ortberg Jr. is teaching pastor at Willow Creek Community Church in South Barrington, Illinois. He is the author of *The Life You've Always Wanted* and *Love Beyond Reason*. John and his wife, Nancy, live in the Chicago area with their three children, Laura, Mallory, and Johnny.

Laurie Pederson, a real estate investment manager, is a founding member of Willow Creek Community Church. As an elder since 1978, she has helped shape many of the foundational values and guiding principles of the church. She is cocreator of Willow Creek's discipleship-based church membership process. Laurie lives outside of Chicago with her husband, Scott.

Judson Poling, a staff member at Willow Creek Community Church since 1980, writes small group training materials and many of the dramas performed in Willow Creek's outreach services. He is coauthor of the *Walking with God* and *Tough Questions* Bible study series and general editor of *The Journey: A Study Bible for Spiritual Seekers*. He lives in Algonquin, Illinois, with his wife, Deb, and their two children, Anna and Ryan.

WILLOW
Willow Creek Association

Willow Creek Association
Vision, Training, Resources for Prevailing Churches

This resource was created to serve you and to help you build a local church that prevails. It is just one of many ministry tools that are part of the Willow Creek Resources® line, published by the Willow Creek Association together with Zondervan.

The Willow Creek Association (WCA) was created in 1992 to serve a rapidly growing number of churches from across the denominational spectrum that are committed to helping unchurched people become fully devoted followers of Christ. Membership in the WCA now numbers over 10,000 Member Churches worldwide from more than ninety denominations.

The Willow Creek Association links like-minded Christian leaders with each other and with strategic vision, training, and resources in order to help them build prevailing churches designed to reach their redemptive potential. Here are some of the ways the WCA does that.

- **Prevailing Church Conference**—an annual two-and-a-half day event, held at Willow Creek Community Church in South Barrington, Illinois, to help pioneering church leaders raise up a volunteer core while discovering new and innovative ways to build prevailing churches that reach unchurched people.

- **Leadership Summit**—a once-a-year, two-and-a-half-day conference to envision and equip Christians with leadership gifts and responsibilities. Presented live at Willow Creek as well as via satellite broadcast to over sixty locations across North America, this event is designed to increase the leadership effectiveness of pastors, ministry staff, volunteer church leaders, and Christians in the marketplace.

- **Ministry-Specific Conferences**—throughout each year the WCA hosts a variety of conferences and training events—both at Willow Creek's main campus and off-site, across the U.S. and around the world—targeting church leaders in ministry-specific areas such as: evangelism, the arts, children, students, small groups, preaching and teaching, spiritual formation, spiritual gifts, raising up resources, etc.

- **Willow Creek Resources®**—to provide churches with trusted and field-tested ministry resources in such areas as leadership, evangelism, spiritual formation, spiritual gifts, small groups, stewardship, student ministry, children's ministry, the use of the arts—drama, media, contemporary music—and more. For additional information about Willow Creek Resources® call the Customer Service Center at 800-570-9812. Outside the U.S. call 847-765-0070.

- *WillowNet*—the WCA's Internet resource service, which provides access to hundreds of transcripts of Willow Creek messages, drama scripts, songs, videos, and multimedia tools. The system allows users to sort through these elements and download them for a fee. Visit us online at www.willowcreek.com.

- *WCA News*—a quarterly publication to inform you of the latest trends, resources, and information on WCA events from around the world.

- *Defining Moments*—a monthly audio journal for church leaders featuring Bill Hybels and other Christian leaders discussing probing issues to help you discover biblical principles and transferable strategies to maximize your church's redemptive potential.

- *The Exchange*—our online classified ads service to assist churches in recruiting key staff for ministry positions.

- **Member Benefits**—includes substantial discounts to WCA training events, a 20 percent discount on all Willow Creek Resources®, access to a Members-Only section on WillowNet, monthly communications, and more. Member Churches also receive special discounts and premier services through WCA's growing number of ministry partners—Select Service Providers.

For specific information about WCA membership, upcoming conferences, and other ministry services contact:

Willow Creek Association
P.O. Box 3188, Barrington, IL 60011-3188
Phone: 847-570-9812
Fax: 847-765-5046
www.willowcreek.com

a place where . . .

nobody stands alone!

Small groups, when they're working right, provide a place where you can experience continuous growth and community—the deepest level of community, modeled after the church in Acts 2, where believers are devoted to Christ's teachings and to fellowship with each other.

If you'd like to take the next step in building that kind of small group environment for yourself or for your church, we'd like to help.

The Willow Creek Association in South Barrington, Illinois, hosts an annual Small Groups Conference attended by thousands of church and small group leaders from around the world. Each year we also lead small group training events and workshops in seven additional cities across the country. We offer a number of small group resources for both small groups and small group leaders available to you through your local bookstore and Willow Creek Resources.

If you'd like to learn more, contact the Willow Creek Association at 1-800-570-9812. Or visit us on-line: www.willowcreek.com.

continue the transformation .

PURSUING SPIRITUAL TRANSFORMATI

JOHN ORTBERG, LAURIE PEDERSON, JUDSON POLING

Experience a radical change in how you think and how yo
live. Forget about trying hard to be a better person. We
come instead to the richly rewarding process of discoverin
and growing into the person God made you to be! Devel
oped by Willow Creek Community Church as its core cur
riculum, this planned, progressive small group approach t
spiritual maturity will help you:

- Become more like Jesus
- Recapture the image of God in your life
- Cultivate intimacy with God
- Live your faith everywhere, all the time
- Renew your zest for life

Leader's guide included!

Fully Devoted:
Living Each Day in Jesus' Name   0-310-22073-4

Grace:
An Invitation to a Way of Life   0-310-22074-2

Growth:
Training vs. Trying   0-310-22075-0

Groups:
The Life-Giving Power of Community   0-310-22076-9

Gifts:
The Joy of Serving God   0-310-22077-7

Giving:
Unlocking the Heart of Good Stewardship   0-310-22078-5

Look for Pursuing Spiritual Transformation *at
your local bookstore.*

WILLOW
Willow Creek Resources

www.willowcreek.com

ZONDERVAN™

GRAND RAPIDS, MICHIGAN 49530 US
WWW.ZONDERVAN.COM

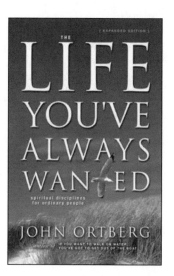

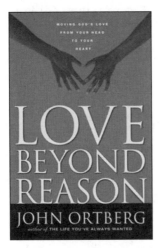